About the Book

The inadequacies of the Continental Congress became painfully apparent during Shays' Rebellion in 1786. People began calling for "a hoop to the barrel"—a strengthened government to serve the republic and to hold the separate states more strongly together.

Fifty-five men, representing twelve of the thirteen states, gathered in Philadelphia the following summer to create a revolutionary document. Referring frequently to historic ideas of liberty and government, they began to debate the many issues before them.

What form should the government take? Who should lead the country? (Alexander Hamilton suggested a king.) Who could run for President? (Some felt only rich men should qualify.) What would his powers be? How could the interests of the small states be represented best?

George Sanderlin brings the Constitutional Convention's personalities, debates, confrontations, and compromises into bold relief with first-hand accounts of the proceedings, and he shows us the difficulties of ratification in the face of the growing demand for a "bill of rights." His skillful selections of source material, bound together by his own succinct narrative, provide a stimulating opportunity to see the dynamics of history in the making. An invaluable, complete reference source.

A NW. VIEW OF THE STATE HOUSE IN PHILADELPHIA taken 1778

A Hoop to the Barrel

The Making of the American Constitution

by GEORGE SANDERLIN

COWARD, McCANN & GEOGHEGAN, INC.
NEW YORK

Cover: William K. Plummer has based his artwork on political cartoons of the period. As soon as a state voted in favor of the Constitution, it was represented by an upstanding pillar, symbolically joined to the states that had previously ratified.

Author's Note

Punctuation and capitalization used in the original source material quoted here has been retained, but spelling has been standardized and long paragraphs have been broken up, for the reader's convenience.

To Ferdinand N. Monjo

Friend and Editor

CONTENTS

CAST OF CHARACTERS

The Leading Delegates

GUNNING BEDFORD. Attorney general of Delaware. Very fat and impetuous; a "bold and nervous Speaker" who defends the small states. Attended Princeton with James Madison.

JOHN DICKINSON. Pale, scholarly lawyer, educated at the Middle Temple, London. Famous for his defense of American rights in *Letters from an American Farmer* (1767–68); now semiretired in Delaware.

OLIVER ELLSWORTH. Tall, successful Connecticut lawyer and businessman, who has a habit of talking to himself. A moderate nationalist with à sure instinct for compromise. (See page 101 for picture.)

BENJAMIN FRANKLIN. World-famous octogenarian of Philadelphia—printer, scientist, diplomat. "He snatched lightning from Heaven and the sceptre from tyrants." Supports a strong Union, envisions a continental republic.

ELBRIDGE GERRY. Thin, dapper merchant from Marblehead, Massachusetts. Worried-looking, veering between republicanism and nationalism, yet sensitive to slights; stubborn in his views of the moment.

NATHANIEL GORHAM. Likable Boston merchant who leans toward nationalism. Son of a packet-boat operator, trained as a mechanic; engaged in privateering during the Revolution.

ELBRIDGE GERRY

GUNNING BEDFORD

JOHN DICKINSON

NATHANIEL GORHAM

BENJAMIN FRANKLIN

ALEXANDER HAMILTON. Brilliant nationalist from New York, eager for the establishment of a "high-toned" government but discouraged by presence of antinationalist colleagues. A short, slender man with mobile features; native of the British West Indies; very ambitious. (See page 80 for picture.)

WILLIAM JOHNSON. Modest, gracious Connecticut lawyer and scholar. Independently wealthy; shuns strife. Educated at Yale and Harvard; has just been named president of Columbia.

RUFUS KING. Good-looking young Massachusetts lawyer; converted to nationalism by his membership in Congress and the influence of Madison. Educated at Harvard; an effective speaker.

JOHN LANSING. Wealthy New York landowner and lawyer. Speaker of the New York assembly and dependable lieutenant of antinationalist Governor Clinton. Handsome, hospitable.

JAMES MADISON. "A small man, quiet, somewhat precise in manner, pleasant, fond of conversation, with a . . . mixture of ease and dignity." A Virginian with a deep knowledge of ancient constitutions, also a sly sense of humor; leader of the nationalists.

LUTHER MARTIN. Carelessly dressed, broad-shouldered Marylander, with hair cropped short and florid complexion. Violently antinationalist; a long-winded orator known as the "reprobate genius" or wild man of the Convention.

WILLIAM JOHNSON

JAMES MADISON

LUTHER MARTIN

RUFUS KING

GEORGE MASON. Independent, outspoken Virginia planter-aristocrat. A romantic republican, author of the Virginia Declaration of Rights; enemy of slavery and centralized government.

GOUVERNEUR MORRIS. "The Tall Boy"—a large, genial, personable man with a peg leg, a strong nationalist from Pennsylvania. Gay, witty, a favorite with the ladies; steeped in French literature and an excellent writer.

ROBERT MORRIS. Hearty, thick-necked Philadelphia businessman known as the Financier of the Revolution. Hosts George Washington during the Convention; faces financial ruin and debtor's prison in the future.

WILLIAM PATERSON. A short, stubborn Irishman; attorney general of New Jersey, Revolutionary veteran. Determined to protect states' rights, though willing to accept a moderate nationalism which does not infringe those rights.

CHARLES COTESWORTH PINCKNEY. South Carolina lawyer-planter; distinguished general during the Revolution, an aide to Washington. Educated at Oxford and the Middle Temple, London. Genial, imposing; highly regarded in South Carolina.

CHARLES PINCKNEY. Second cousin to General Pinckney. A dedicated nationalist, lawyer, prominent member of Congress. Youthful, but wishes to be thought still younger than his twenty-nine years; handsome, somewhat vain.

GEORGE MASON

WILLIAM PATERSON

ROBERT MORRIS

GOUVERNEUR MORRIS

CHARLES COTESWORTH PINCKNEY

EDMUND RANDOLPH. Handsome, dark-haired governor of Virginia. A moderate nationalist, but concerned about his popularity and political standing at home. Educated at William and Mary.

JOHN RUTLEDGE. Proud, imperious South Carolina planter-aristocrat. Activist-leader in his state during the Revolution. Educated at the Middle Temple, London.

ROGER SHERMAN. Lean, sharp-nosed, canny New Englander; jack-of-all-trades who has risen from a shoemaker's to a judge's bench in Connecticut. Inclines slightly toward antinationalism, but is pragmatic. Called "cunning as the Devil" by an opponent.

GEORGE WASHINGTON. Powerfully built—six feet four inches tall, weighs 220 pounds. Controls his strong feelings; lives by maxims of truth and honor; hates to be the object of criticisms ("animadversions"). Speaks only twice during the Convention but keeps the delegates in order by his awesome presence. (See page 23 for picture.)

HUGH WILLIAMSON. Scientist, physician (MD from Utrecht), surgeon-general of the North Carolina forces during the Revolution. A very versatile, genial man of the world; a strong nationalist.

JAMES WILSON. "The Caledonian" [Scotsman]—stout, ruddy, precise. Educated at St. Andrews University, Scotland, before coming to Pennsylvania as a country lawyer. Powerful champion of the nationalists; noted for his reasoning ability.

JAMES WILSON

JOHN RUTLEDGE

ROGER SHERMAN

EDMUND RANDOLPH

HUGH WILLIAMSON

Counselors and Critics

JOHN ADAMS. Blunt, honest Massachusetts lawyer, states-
man, and leader of the Revolution. Overseas, during
the Convention, serving as ambassador to England,
but keenly interested. Author of a pamphlet,
Thoughts on Government (1776), and the Massachusetts constitution (1779)—basic documents ad-
vocating and carrying out limited, representative
government with a separation of the powers.

WILLIAM GRAYSON. Distinguished Virginia lawyer who
considered the Constitution "a most ridiculous piece
of business." Educated in England, with military experience in Europe. Battles against ratification of the
Constitution in Virginia with rapier wit, as well as
sound arguments.

PATRICK HENRY. Fiery orator of the Revolution—gaunt,
deep-voiced, with a habit of twirling his wig several
times around his head at crucial points in a speech.
A self-educated lawyer from the Virginia backwoods who leads the fight against ratification of the
Constitution in that state. (See page 64 for picture.)

THOMAS JEFFERSON. Champion of political and religious
liberty; wartime governor of Virginia; author of
the Declaration of Independence. Now ambassador
to France, but keeps in touch with the Convention
through correspondence with James Madison. Vi-
vacious, warmhearted, talented in all fields; advocates a bill of rights for the Constitution. (See page 45
for picture.)

JOHN ADAMS

WILLIAM GRAYSON

PROLOGUE

In 1787, Americans were bursting with energy. They were busy building bridges, digging canals, inventing steamboats. Many were streaming across the Appalachians to settle America's big backyard, between the mountains and the Mississippi.

But a stumbling Congress which had no real power cast a shadow over the future. Each state was independent; it could quarrel with its neighbor, or tax its neighbor's goods, or print too much paper money and cause an inflation. Northerners fought with Southerners over slavery and tariffs. Backcountry men were suspicious of seaboard lawyers and merchants. Two mighty empires—Great Britain and Spain—hemmed the young nation in and threatened its growth.

It was in this atmosphere of uncertainty and conflict that fifty-five delegates assembled in the rainy spring in Philadelphia. Chosen by their state legislatures, they had the task of saving the American Republic by revising the weak Articles of Confederation.

They met in the big square east room of the State House—high-ceilinged, gray-paneled. Perspiring in their tight wigs and woolen waistcoats, they labored, three or four at a table, on a new plan. At the east end of the room, on a raised platform, sat their chairman, a tall Virginian in a blue military coat. By the end of the summer they had produced a document which began: "We the People of the United States. . . ."

This was a new phrase. Not "the people of New York"

19

or "the sovereign state of Maryland" but "We the People of the United States." It marked the birth of a new government—a new nation. It was the preamble of a Constitution which safeguarded liberty by checks and balances but established unity through the supremacy of the federal government. When the first ten amendments, known as the Bill of Rights, were added, this document would inspire democratic reforms around the world.

The Constitutional Convention was a more sober gathering than the defiant wartime Congresses, yet it was called "an assembly of demigods" by Thomas Jefferson. The names of its members read like a roll call of American history: George Washington, Benjamin Franklin, James Madison, Alexander Hamilton, George Mason, James Wilson, Roger Sherman, John Rutledge, Edmund Randolph, Rufus King, Gouverneur Morris—to mention just a few.

But the Constitution, which George Washington called a "miracle," was by no means guaranteed completion or ratification. If the delegates had labored less stubbornly, if the crises of that humid summer had not been overcome, there would have been no Constitution. A strengthened Republic with a continental destiny might never have come into being.

The hope for such a Republic, as well as for the liberties declared in 1776, was at stake in that east room, whose lofty windows could not be opened because of the flies angrily buzzing outside. Slatted blinds kept out the summer sun, but the air was stale and lifeless. At the most critical stage of the Convention the crashing thunderstorms which briefly cooled the afternoons did not break.

Yet the delegates struggled on, as we shall see. Strongminded men clashed, hammered out compromises or departed, did not "leak" what they were doing, sometimes returned. . . . Their goal was not military glory or a famous voyage of discovery, but to construct a government for free men. Nor were cannon fired or bells rung at the end of this journey, September 17, 1787.

There was only a slender sheaf of parchment, white against the green baize cloth of the chairman's table. There were only the weary signers crowding around, not knowing whether the nation would accept or reject what they had labored for.

This was the American Constitution—the charter of what is today the oldest democratic government on earth but was then only a precarious experiment in the New World wilderness. The pages that follow tell its story, which is the story of the men—dashing, eccentric, witty, profound, human—who made it.

CAN AMERICA
GOVERN ITSELF?

. . . unless the States will suffer Congress to
exercise those prerogatives, they are undoubtedly invested with by the Constitution [the
Articles of Confederation], every thing must
very rapidly tend to Anarchy and confusion. . . .
—GEORGE WASHINGTON

BENJAMIN FRANKLIN'S DREAM

In 1754 Europe stood on the brink of its first world war. The conflict among England, France, and Spain was about to spread to the New World, and there was a restless stirring, from the heights of Quebec to the Florida lagoons. Which flag would eventually fly over eastern North America—the Union Jack, the French lilies, or the red and yellow banners of Castile?

The imminent danger to the British colonies came from the French and their Indian allies. The French held Canada and the territory just beyond the Appalachians, the back fence of the colonies. They threatened to break through.

Or, to look at it from the French point of view, the problem was the exploding population of the British colonies. Scores of land seekers spilled over the mountains into the Ohio country claimed by the French. These unwelcome newcomers threatened to cut the line of communications between French Canada and French Louisiana. To prevent this, France had just built a chain of log forts along the Allegheny and upper Ohio Rivers.

As for Spain, it watched both sides anxiously. Florida, Texas, and New Mexico were the northern ramparts of the far-flung Spanish empire—but Spain was busy preparing contingency plans, also, for the take-over of the Mississippi Valley.

In this time of alarms for the British colonies the most original counsel was given by a successful Philadelphia printer and scientist, Benjamin Franklin. Franklin's countrymen tended to think only of their own colonies. But this driving entrepreneur with the bold eyes and firm chin had a vision of an America whose mountains, plains, and forests would become the future stronghold of the English-speaking people. His countrymen were preoccupied with colonial disputes—but Franklin dreamed of colonial union.

He not only printed the first American political cartoon, exhorting the colonies—shown as parts of a dismembered snake—to "Join, or Die," but also sketched a plan for a more or less autonomous British American government representing all the colonies. The Albany Congress of seven Northern colonies, meeting in June, 1754, to discuss defense, recommended Franklin's scheme to the colonies for adoption.

But the colonies would have none of it. No colonial assembly would allow a higher body—a grand council representing all the colonies—to untie the purse strings of its constituents and collect taxes. Franklin's own Pennsylvania Assembly even waited until he was absent, then rejected it.

The colonies were too selfish to achieve self-rule.

So the plan was never presented to Parliament by the colonies. But if it had been, Parliament would probably have been suspicious of it also. British officials were having enough trouble with headstrong assemblies of individual colonies; they would not have welcomed confrontations with a superassembly of cantankerous colonials.

Franklin himself always believed that if the plan had been accepted, the American Revolution would at least have been postponed. The following selection tells about the plan and its fate; the passage is from his *Autobiography* (written 1771–1790, first complete edition 1867).

In 1754, War with France being again apprehended, a Congress of Commissioners from the different Colonies was, by an Order of the Lords of Trade, to be assembled at Albany, there to confer with the Chiefs of the Six Nations, concerning the Means of defending both their Country and ours. Governor Hamilton [of Pennsylvania] . . . [named] my self, to join Mr. Thomas Penn and Mr. Secretary Peters, as Commissioners to act for Pennsylvania. . . .

In our Way thither [to Albany], I projected and drew up a Plan for the Union of all the Colonies, under one Government so far as might be necessary for Defense, and other important general Purposes. As we pass'd thro' New York, I had there shown my Project to Mr. James Alexander and Mr. Kennedy, two Gentlemen of great Knowledge in public Affairs, and being fortified by their Approbation I ventur'd to lay it before the Congress. It then appear'd that several of the Commissioners had form'd Plans of the same kind. A previous Question was first taken whether a Union should be established, which pass'd in the Affirmative unanimously.

A Committee was then appointed one Member from each Colony, to consider the several Plans and report. Mine happen'd to be prefer'd, and with a few Amendments was accordingly reported. By this Plan, the general Government was to be administered by a President General appointed and supported by the Crown, and a Grand Council to be chosen by the Representatives of the People of the several Colonies met in their respective Assemblies. The Debates upon it in Congress went on daily hand in hand with the Indian Business. Many Objections and Difficulties were started, but at length they were all overcome, and the Plan was unanimously agreed to, and Copies ordered to be transmitted to the Board of Trade and to the Assemblies of the several Provinces.

Its Fate was singular. The Assemblies did not adopt it as they all thought there was too much *Prerogative* [power of the British Crown] in it; and in England it was judg'd to have too much of the *Democratic*: The Board of Trade therefore did not approve of it; nor recommend it for the Approbation of his Majesty; but another Scheme was form'd (suppos'd better to answer the same Purpose) whereby the Governors of the Provinces with some Members of their respective Councils were to meet and order the raising of Troops, building of Forts, &c. &c. to draw on the Treasury of Great Britain for the Expense, which was afterwards to be refunded by an Act of Parliament laying a Tax on America. . . .

Being the Winter following in Boston, I had much Conversation with Govr. Shirley [of Massachusetts] upon both the Plans. . . . The different and contrary Reasons of dislike to my Plan, makes me suspect that it was really the true Medium; and I am still of Opinion it would have been happy for both Sides the Water if it had been adopted. The Colonies so united would have been sufficiently strong to have defended themselves; there would then have been no need of Troops from England; of course the subsequent Pretence for Taxing America, and the bloody Contest it occasioned, would have been avoided. But such Mistakes are not new; History is full of the Errors of States and Princes.

"*Look round the habitable World, how few*
Know their own Good, or knowing it pursue."

Those who govern, having much Business on their hands, do not generally like to take the Trouble of considering and carrying into Execution new Projects. The best public Measures are therefore seldom *adopted from previous Wisdom, but forc'd by the Occasion.*

A "LEAGUE OF FRIENDSHIP"

Five years after Benjamin Franklin's Albany Plan was rejected, a thin red line of British soldiers stood on the Plains of Abraham, outside Quebec, facing the advancing "battalions of Old France, a torrent of white uniforms and gleaming bayonets." Here, on September 13, 1759, young James Wolfe won a continent for Great Britain.

The colonies helped, some more than others, in Britain's Seven Years' War against France and its allies. But when France ceded Canada to England, in 1763, the colonists gained more than they had invested. Suddenly, they were freed of the fear of a powerful neighbor. Their western frontier was transformed from a barrier to a gateway, leading to the fertile Ohio lands. And their dependence on the distant British Parliament was dramatically lessened. If they wished—and if they could at last unite—they might even defy that Parliament and its king.

This, of course, is what happened. For just when conditions made independence possible, Britain decided to make new rules for the colonies and to enforce old ones strictly. The Stamp Act did more than Benjamin Franklin had been able to do to bring the colonies together. Further conflicts led to the American Revolution and the Declaration of Independence. Then the former colonies had to draw up a plan by which to govern themselves.

They didn't quite succeed. The Articles of Confederation, ratified in 1781, merely legalized the wartime *voluntary* cooperation between the states. The Articles provided for a "league of friendship" or gentleman's agreement among the parties. The states remained sovereign; Congress had as much or as little power as it was their whim to give it. There was no strong executive to attempt to increase the authority of the central government.

Nor could the system be strengthened by amendments —since no amendment could be adopted without the unanimous approval of all the states. "Each state retains its sovereignty, freedom, and independence," proclaimed little Rhode Island as it vetoed one important amendment. New York rejected a later, even more crucial one.

Worst of all, Congress could neither tax Americans nor collect duties on imported goods. It depended on "requisitions"—requests for money from the individual states, which those states were free to ignore. When Congress received news of the victory at Yorktown, there was not enough money in the treasury to pay the messenger's expenses; each member had to contribute a dollar out of his own pocket!

The nation—as distinct from the states—had not yet achieved responsible self-rule.

The Articles of Confederation did give Congress control of the unsettled Western lands. And it was at this time that Congress adopted the eagle of imperial Rome— in place of the wild turkey Benjamin Franklin wanted— as the nation's symbol. But Alexander Hamilton, ambitious and farseeing,, spoke for many shrewd observers when he declared that unless Congress were given more power, the hope for "a great Federal Republic" would be lost. (For the complete Articles of Confederation, under which the United States was governed from 1781 to 1787, see pp. 177-87.)

WASHINGTON'S WARNING

As the American Revolution was ending, the soldiers threatened to mutiny because they had not been paid. Once the hapless Congress of the victorious Republic even had to flee from Philadelphia to Princeton to escape the disorderly veterans.

George Washington was deeply troubled both by the misconduct of the soldiers and by a growing selfishness among civilians. Like his young favorite Hamilton, Washington suspected that the Articles of Confederation might not be strong enough to bind the states together. One of his last acts as commander in chief was to urge his fellow citizens "to forget their local prejudices and policies." They should place first "the general prosperity"— what was good for the whole nation.

The following selection, containing this warning, is from George Washington's letter to the governors, 1783 (from Forrest McDonald and Ellen Shapiro McDonald, *Confederation and Constitution 1781–1789*).

There are four things, which I humbly conceive, are essential to the well being, I may even venture to say, to the existence of the United States as an Independent Power:

1st. An indissoluble Union of the States under one Federal Head.

2dly. A Sacred regard to Public Justice.

3dly. The adoption of a proper Peace Establishment, and

4thly. The prevalence of that pacific and friendly Disposition, among the People of the United States, which will induce them to forget their local prejudices and policies, to make those mutual concessions which are requisite to the general prosperity, and in some instances, to sacrifice their individual advantages to the interest of the Community....

Under the first head, altho' it may not be necessary or proper for me in this place ... to take up the great question . . . whether it be expedient and requisite for the States to delegate a larger proportion of Power to Congress, or not. Yet it will be a part of my duty . . . to insist upon the following positions:

That unless the States will suffer Congress to exercise those prerogatives, they are undoubtedly invested with by the Constitution [the Articles of Confederation], every thing must very rapidly tend to Anarchy and confusion; That it is indispensable to the happiness of the individual States, that there should be lodged somewhere, a Supreme Power to regulate and govern the general concerns of the Confederated Republic . . . ; That there must be a faithful and pointed compliance on the part of every State, with the late proposals and demands of Congress, or the most fatal consequences will ensue; That whatever measures have a tendency to dissolve the Union, or . . . lessen the Sovereign Authority, ought to be considered as hostile to the Liberty and Independency of America . . . ; and lastly, that unless we can be enabled by the concurrence of the States, to participate of the fruits of the Revolution, and enjoy the essential benefits of Civil Society, under a form of Government so free and uncorrupted . . . as has been devised and adopted by the Articles of Confederation, it will be a subject of regret, that . . . so many sacrifices have been made in vain.

In the postwar confusion, there were a few bright spots. One was the movement toward the abolition of slavery.

Just before the Revolution, patriotic Americans had been organizing as Sons of Liberty. But an English Tory like Dr. Samuel Johnson could ask sarcastically how free were the black Americans—the slaves who made up nearly one-fifth of the population.

In 1783 Massachusetts answered Dr. Johnson. A white man, Nathaniel Jennison, was arrested for beating a black named Quock Walker. Jennison's defense was that Walker was merely a slave—his property. Walker argued that the Massachusetts constitution of 1780, which stated that all men are born free and equal, had in effect abolished slavery.

In the following selection, Chief Justice Caleb Cushing, of the Massachusetts Supreme Court, considers these arguments and hands down his decision. The verdict in this case ended slavery in Massachusetts. (From Forrest McDonald and Ellen Shapiro McDonald, *Confederation and Constitution 1781–1789*).

Quock Walker v. Nathaniel Jennison (1783)

As to the doctrine of slavery and the right of Christians to hold Africans in perpetual servitude, and sell and treat them as we do our horses and cattle, that (it is true) has been heretofore countenanced by the Province Laws formerly, but nowhere is it expressly enacted or established. It has been a usage—a usage which took its origin from the practice of some of the European nations, and the regulations of British government respecting the then Colonies, for the benefit of trade and wealth.

But whatever sentiments have formerly prevailed in this particular or slid in upon us by the example of others, a different idea has taken place with the people of America, more favorable to the natural rights of mankind, and to that natural, innate desire of Liberty, with which Heaven (without regard to color, complexion, or shape of noses—features) has inspired all the human race. And upon this ground our Constitution of Government, by which the people of this Commonwealth have solemnly bound themselves, sets out with declaring that all men are born free and equal—and that every subject is entitled to liberty, and to have it guarded by the laws, as well as life and property—and in short is totally repugnant to the idea of being born slaves.

This being the case, I think the idea of slavery is inconsistent with our own conduct and Constitution; and there can be no such thing as perpetual servitude of a rational creature, unless his liberty is forfeited by some criminal conduct or given up by personal consent or contract. . . . *Verdict Guilty.*

FREEDOM OF CONSCIENCE

Three years after the Quock Walker case, the Virginia Assembly struck a blow for religious liberty.

The idea of an established church, backed by the power of the state, had been accepted in the Middle Ages and had even been strengthened by some aspects of the Protestant Reformation. But eighteenth-century rationalists like Thomas Jefferson argued for a separation of church and state. In 1786 the Virginia Assembly became one of the first legislative bodies of the New World—or the Old World—to realize this ideal.

The following selection is from the Virginia Act for Establishing Religious Freedom, January 16, 1786 (from Forrest McDonald and Ellen Shapiro McDonald, *Confederation and Constitution 1781–1789*).

WHEREAS Almighty God hath created the mind free; that all attempts to influence it by temporal punishments or burthens, or by civil incapacitations, tend only to beget habits of hypocrisy and meanness, and are a departure from the plan of the Holy Author of our religion, Who . . . chose not to propagate it by coercions. . . .

Be it enacted by the General Assembly. That no man shall be compelled to frequent or support any religious worship, place, or ministry whatsoever, nor shall be enforced, restrained, molested, or burthened in his body or goods, nor shall otherwise suffer on account of his religious opinions or belief; but that all men shall be free to profess, and by argument to maintain, their opinion in matters of religion, and that the same shall in no wise diminish, enlarge, or affect their civil capacities.

And though we well know that this assembly . . . have no power to restrain the acts of succeeding assemblies . . . yet we are free to declare, and do declare, that the rights hereby asserted are of the natural rights of mankind, and that if any act shall be hereafter passed to repeal the present, or to narrow its operation, such act will be an infringement of natural right.

A FLOOD OF IMPORTS

An independent America encountered trade barriers against its goods everywhere in Europe—not to mention low-slung black pirate vessels in the Mediterranean which seized Yankee ships. Yet the growing Republic wanted, and needed, many essential foreign goods. Because of the imports they purchased, Americans soon found themselves short of hard cash and deep in debt.

America's ambassador to Britain, bluff John Adams, tried to remedy this situation by urging the British to lower their tariffs against our goods, so we could sell more overseas. (England sent us twice as many products as we sent it.) Adams presented the American case for freer trade to Prime Minister William Pitt—but without much success.

The following selection is from John Adams' report to John Jay, August 25, 1785 (from Forrest McDonald and Ellen Shapiro McDonald, *Confederation and Constitution 1781–1789*).

I will be very frank with you [Mr. Pitt], sir, said I, and I think it will be best for us to go to the bottom of these subjects. The Americans think that their exclusion from your West India Islands, the refusal of their ships and oil and other things, and their exclusion from your Colonies on the continent and Newfoundland, discover [reveal] a jealousy of their little naval power, and a fixed system of policy to prevent the growth of it; and this is an idea that they cannot bear.

No, said he, if we endeavored to lessen your shipping and seamen, without benefiting or increasing our own, it would be hard and unreasonable . . . but when we only aim at making the most of our own . . . you cannot justly complain.

I am happy, sir, to hear you avow this principle, and agree with you perfectly in it; let us apply it. Both parties having the right and the power to confine their exports and imports to their own ships and seamen, if both exercise the right and exert the power in its full extent, what is the effect? The commerce must cease between them. Is this eligible [acceptable] for either?

To be sure, said he, we should well consider the advantages and the disadvantages in such a case.

If it is not found to be eligible for either, said I, after having well considered, what remains, but that we should agree upon a liberal plan, and allow equal freedom to each other's ships and seamen? especially if it should be found that this alone can preserve friendship and good humor. For I fully believe that this plan alone can ever put this nation in good humor with America, or America with this country.

CLOSE THE MISSISSIPPI?

In 1786, Spain offered the storm-tossed young Republic a tempting passage to riches. Having closed the Mississippi to American navigation in 1784, Spain wished to make this closing permanent. If the United States would surrender its claim to sail down the great river, Spain would open its ports to American goods.

These "castles in Spain" would be sources of real wealth. New England fish and manufactures, Middle States wheat, Southern tobacco could go not only to

Spain's Caribbean islands but to the "metropolis"—populous Spain itself—almost duty-free.

On the other hand, if the United States gave up its claim to navigate the Mississippi, it would be abandoning its dream of westward expansion. Nationalist-minded members of Congress did not hesitate to attack the Spanish offer. Neither did Southern members, who represented speculators in Western lands.

In the end, the proposed treaty was rejected. If it had passed, the adventurer James Wilkinson might have succeeded in his efforts to persuade Kentuckians to become subjects of Spain! The American Republic would have found itself walled in, as the colonies had once been, by the Appalachians. Even with the treaty refused, the formidable Spanish empire still blocked the roads west, and Spain was an opponent the weak Confederation Congress would not challenge.

A BANKRUPT CONGRESS—
THE NORTHWEST ORDINANCE

At the very moment that Congress was rejecting the Spanish offer, it was nearly bankrupt. Its handful of soldiers in the Northwest were clamoring for their pay. Foreign governments demanded the interest due on their loans. But Congress could scarcely pay the bills for its own expenses, such as rent and paper.

One state after another "refused a compliance" to the requisitions (requests for money) from Congress. In desperation, Congress turned to the one resource it possessed. Its cupboard might be bare, but at least it was "land poor." Maryland had insisted that all the states turn their Western lands over to Congress before it accepted the Articles of Confederation.

In 1785 Congress decided to sell the land north of the Ohio River. And in 1787 Jefferson's original plan of 1784, with modifications, was passed as the Northwest Ordinance. This was the most important law made under the Articles of Confederation.

The keynote of the Northwest Ordinance was *equality*. Each of the three to five states into which the territory would be divided would come into the Union fully equal to the older states. Even the word "territory" was chosen to carry out the ideal of equality, since to Americans who had fought George III the word "colony" suggested inferiority. The establishment of schools was encouraged as an aid toward equality of opportunity. Above all, as in Jefferson's original plan, slavery was forever prohibited here.

Two of the new states, Michigan and Illinois, were eventually given names like ones that Jefferson had suggested. Jefferson's other proposed names—including Assenisipia, Cherroneus, and Metropotomia(!)—were, however, forgotten.

The following selection is from the Northwest Ordinance of 1787, which set the pattern for all future territorial expansion of the United States (from Forrest McDonald and Ellen Shapiro McDonald, *Confederation and Constitution 1781–1789*).

ARTICLE I

No person, demeaning himself in a peaceable and orderly manner, shall ever be molested on account of his mode of worship, or religious sentiments, in the said territory.

ARTICLE II

The inhabitants of the said territory shall always be entitled to the benefits of the writs of *habeas cor-*

pus, and of the trial by jury; of a proportionate representation of the people in the legislature, and of judicial proceedings according to the course of the common law. All persons shall be bailable, unless for capital offenses, where the proof shall be evident, or the presumption great. All fines shall be moderate; and no cruel or unusual punishment shall be inflicted. No man shall be deprived of his liberty or property, but by the judgment of his peers, or the law of the land. . . .

ARTICLE III

Religion, morality, and knowledge being necessary to good government and the happiness of mankind, schools and the means of education shall forever be encouraged. The utmost good faith shall always be observed towards the Indians; their lands and property shall never be taken from them without their consent. . . .

ARTICLE V

There shall be formed in the said territory not less than three nor more than five States . . . And whenever any of the said States shall have sixty thousand free inhabitants therein, such States shall be admitted by its delegates, into the Congress of the United States, on an equal footing with the original States, in all respects whatever; and shall be at liberty to form a permanent constitution and State government: *Provided*, The constitution and government, so to be formed, shall be republican, and in conformity to the principles contained in these articles. . . .

ARTICLE VI

There shall be neither slavery nor involuntary servitude in the said territory, otherwise than in the punishment of crimes, whereof the party shall have been duly convicted: *Provided always*, That any person escaping into the same, from whom labor or service is lawfully claimed in any one of the original States, such fugitive may be lawfully reclaimed, and conveyed to the person claiming his or her labor or service.

REBELLION IN MASSACHUSETTS

The Confederation Congress had not really solved any of its most pressing problems—the unfavorable balance of trade, the poor finances, the absenteeism of its members, the disrespect shown it by the states. No help could be expected from the settlement of the Northwest Territory until some years had passed. Overseas, the Barbary pirates continued their attacks on American shipping unchecked.

Nevertheless, the government was muddling through—until a rebellion broke out in western Massachusetts which shocked the nation.

In that rural section the effects of the depression and money shortage had been severe. And the ruling merchant class in Boston had refused to allow the printing of paper money, with which the farmers might have paid their bills. Creditors went to court to claim men's lands in payment for their debts—and in the fall of 1786 farmers revolted.

Angrily, they seized pitchforks and staves and broke up the courts. They proclaimed that they were rebelling against "the present expensive mode of collecting debts, which by reason of the great scarcity of cash, will of necessity fill our gaols [jails] with unhappy debtors . . . a reputable body of people rendered incapable of being serviceable either to themselves or the community."

They also protested against "a suspension of the writ of Habeas Corpus, by which those persons who have stepped forth to assert and maintain the rights of the people, are liable to be taken and conveyed even to the most distant parts of the Commonwealth, and thereby subjected to an unjust punishment."

As their leader, they chose a plain farmer like themselves, the veteran Captain Daniel Shays—who could not pay a debt of $12! Behind Shays, 2,000 ragged but honest men, with rifles in their hands and sprigs of evergreen stuck in their hats, marched on the Springfield arsenal.

Massachusetts sent a frantic appeal to Congress for aid. But Congress could provide neither money nor men. So General Benjamin Lincoln was placed in charge of 4,000 Massachusetts troops. Before Lincoln could reach Springfield, however, Shays and his farmers were there—face to face with General William Shepard and the local militia.

The following selection, from General William Shepard's letter to Governor James Bowdoin, January 26, 1787, tells what happened when these two forces met (from Forrest McDonald and Ellen Shapiro McDonald, *Confederation and Constitution 1781–1789*).

Sir,

The unhappy time is come in which we have been obliged to shed blood. Shays, who was at the head of about twelve hundred men, marched yesterday afternoon about four o'clock, towards the public buildings, in battle array.—He marched his men in an open column by platoons. I sent several times by one of my Aids, and two other gentlemen, Captains Buffington and Woodbridge, to him to know what he was after, or what he wanted. His reply was, He wanted barracks, and barracks he would have, and stores. The answer returned was, He must purchase them dear, if he had them.

He still proceeded on his march, until he approached within two hundred and fifty yards of the arsenal. He then made a halt. I immediately sent Major Lyman, one of my Aids, and Capt. Buffington to inform him not to march his troops any nearer the arsenal on his peril, as I was stationed here by order of your Excellency and the Secretary of War, for the defence of the public property; in case he did, I should surely fire on him and his men. A Mr. Wheeler, who appeared to be one of Shays' Aids, met Mr. Lyman, after he had delivered my orders in the most peremptory manner, and made answer, that that was all he wanted. Mr. Lyman returned with his answer.

Shays immediately put his troops in motion, and marched on rapidly near one hundred yards. I then ordered Major Stephens, who commanded the artillery, to fire upon them, he accordingly did. The two first shot he endeavoured to over-shoot them, in hopes they would have taken warning without firing among them, but it had no effect on them. Major Stephens then directed his shot thro' the centre of his column. The fourth or fifth shot put the whole column into the utmost confusion. Shays made an attempt to display the column, but in vain. We had one howit which was loaded with grape shot, which, when fired, gave them great uneasiness. Had I been disposed to destroy them, I might have charged upon their rear and flanks, with my infantry and the two field-pieces, and could have killed the greater part of his whole army within twenty-five minutes. There was not a single musket fired on either side.

I found three men dead on the spot, and one wounded, who is since dead. One of our artillerymen, by inattention, was badly wounded.

Three muskets were taken up with the dead,

which were all deeply loaded. I have received no reinforcement yet, and expect to be attacked this day by their whole force combined.

"A HOOP TO THE BARREL"

A second attack did not come. The farmers fled, and Shays, after one more skirmish, escaped to the sanctuary of Vermont, which was not yet a member of the Union.

Nevertheless, Shays' Rebellion sent a shudder through the states, from Boston to Savannah. Samuel Adams, the old revolutionist, wanted to hang the new revolutionists. Noah Webster, author of the first American dictionary, decided that America had better have a king after all. Even George Washington, who usually controlled his powerful feelings, was "mortified beyond expression" by the news.

If civil war threatened, the rules would *have* to be changed. "You great men," a simple soldier had urged some time earlier, "[must] have a convention of the States to form a better constitution." In September, 1786, James Madison and Alexander Hamilton had pushed through a resolution in Annapolis, at a meeting about interstate commerce, calling for a convention in Philadelphia to revise the Articles of Confederation.

Now, with the Massachusetts bloodshed and with rumors that some New Yorkers wanted to secede and join Canada, the Confederation Congress at last acted. It summoned its waning powers, rounded up a quorum, and, in effect, issued its own death warrant. It called for a constitutional convention. Such a convention would attempt to provide what many were now demanding: "a hoop to the barrel," a strengthened government to preserve the Republic.

The following selection gives the resolution passed by Congress (from Max Farrand, ed., *The Records of the Federal Convention of 1787*, III).

1787, February 21.

Whereas there is provision in the Articles of Confederation & perpetual Union for making alterations therein by the Assent of a Congress of the United States and of the legislatures of the several States; And whereas experience hath evinced that there are defects in the present Confederation. . . .

Resolved that in the opinion of Congress it is expedient that on the second Monday in May next a Convention of delegates who shall have been appointed by the several states be held at Philadelphia for the sole and express purpose of revising the Articles of Confederation and reporting to Congress and the several legislatures such alterations and provisions as shall when agreed to in Congress and confirmed by the states render the federal constitution adequate to the exigencies of Government & the preservation of the Union.

PHILADELPHIA–
THE CURTAIN RISES

*The Federal convention . . . is really an
assembly of demigods.*

—Thomas Jefferson

CONVENTION CITY

By the end of the bitter-cold winter of 1786–87, fifty-five delegates had been chosen by their state legislatures for the Constitutional Convention. Early in May, they began to arrive in Philadelphia. They found themselves in the business and social capital of the infant republic—a town of nearly 40,000, with small brick and wood houses and wide streets, laid out on a tongue of land between two rivers.

Ships crowded its wharves, heavy wagons clattered over the cobblestones of the treelined streets, lighted at night by Benjamin Franklin's lamps. Sober Quakers in brown and bustling tradesmen, backcountry farmers and European tourists jostled the delegates as they strolled along the raised brick sidewalks. All day long bells rang— for market, for churches, for hawkers of goods. At night the watchman's lonely cry pierced the silence: "Two o'clock—all's clear!"

A handful of Swedes had settled here first, in 1638. But by 1681 the land had come under the control of William Penn, whose agents were told to find a place where the Delaware River was "most navigable, high, dry and healthy; that is, where most ships can best ride, of deepest draught of water." The city was laid out in 1682.

A half century later the State House was begun. In 1787, it appeared as a rectangular red brick building on Chestnut Street, not far from the Schuylkill River. Behind it were green gardens intersected by serpentine gravel paths. From it a famous bell with the Biblical inscription "Proclaim liberty throughout all the land unto all the inhabitants thereof" had pealed loud and long on July 4, 1776.

The following selection gives one tourist's impressions of Philadelphia in the 1780's, including a brief sketch of the Quakers, who fascinated Europeans. The selection is from the *Diary* of Francisco de Miranda, Spanish soldier of fortune and later revolutionary ruler of Venezuela (from Francisco de Miranda, *The New Democracy in America*, tr. by Judson P. Wood).

This city [Philadelphia] is indisputably the largest and most beautiful on this continent. Its streets are straight and are cut at right angles; their width is generally fifty feet (and Market Street one hundred feet), with brick sidewalks on both sides so that people on foot may pass, for which reason little use is made of coaches and carriages. At intervals in front of the houses, forming pillars on the sidewalks, are wooden pumps, which with the greatest convenience and cleanliness supply the inhabitants with all the water they need.

Philadelphia is located at the confluence of the Delaware and Schuylkill rivers, in a dry and dominant spot. Nine streets, which run from one river to the other, intersected perpendicularly by nineteen others, form the center. The houses are comfortable, clean, and in good taste, although somewhat small; they generally have gardens and their architecture is plain and simple, like the dress and habits of the first inhabitants.

It has numerous very good wharves for the facility of commerce; the principal one is two hundred feet wide. The market, the House of Assembly (where the Congress almost always convened for the great work of independence), the hospital, the jail, and the barracks are the principal buildings, constructed with middling skill and with no ornament or decoration whatsoever. The beef market is the best, cleanest, and most abundant I have ever seen; decent women are wont to go to it in the morning and bring home pieces of beef in their hands, without soiling themselves or giving off any bad odor . . . such is the propriety and cleanliness with which everything is regulated!

Christ, St. Peter, and St. Paul are the best churches, and their architecture judicious; the interiors are clean and have iron stoves, which are of infinite help in winter. The church of the Papists is small, but clean and well regulated. . . .

The principal church of the Quakers . . . is on Market Street near the City Hall. Its architecture is greatly lacking in elegance and ornament. There are benches in all parts for the comfort of the congregation; a . . . gallery, for the patented preachers . . . ; a section for the women; and on the walls and pillars some tin-plate candle-holders with wax candles, which give a dark illumination when the night services are celebrated. . . .

I attended the night service, which begins at six o'clock and ends at eight, at one of the Quaker churches. The entire congregation was seated on the benches, their hats on, heads inclined, in the greatest silence. Suddenly the man on my left stands up and in an emphatic tone says, "My spirit says that God shall not always tread upon earth! Because he is in heaven!" Shortly thereafter one of the principal preachers (my neighbor, one supposes, was only a beginner), taking as his text the proverb that says

48

"Think twice and lead once," thrust upon us a sermon lasting more than an hour and a half, in the style of our hebdomadary monks. Another lugubrious and emphatic voice, seemingly that of a woman, recited the Common Prayer; then, all standing up, they shook hands, using the expression "friend," and we all left the church, men and women promiscuously [mixed together]. . . .

The cleanliness, evenness, and length of the streets, their illumination at nighttime, and the vigilance of the guards, posted at each corner to maintain security and good order, make Philadelphia one of the most pleasant and well-ordered cities in the world.

Miranda happened to witness a visit of George Washington to Philadelphia. Here are his impressions of General Washington.

[When] General Washington entered Philadelphia . . . children, men, and women expressed such contentment as if the Redeemer had entered Jerusalem! Such are the excessive fancies and sublime estimation which this fortunate and singular man enjoys in the entire continent. . . .

His manner is circumspect, taciturn, and has little expression, but tranquility and great moderation make him tolerable. I was never able to see him set aside these qualities, despite the fact that the wine flowed with humor and merriment after dinner and that, when drinking certain toasts, he would stand up and give his three cheers with the rest of us. It was not easy to form a definite opinion of his character, and so we will suspend judgment for now.

UNPREDICTABLE NEW ENGLANDERS

Among the delegates straggling into Philadelphia through the rainy month of May, and later, were nine New Englanders. Massachusetts, leader of the Revolution sent four, Connecticut three, and distant New Hampshire two. But Rhode Island, fearful that a strong central government would ban its inflationary paper money, was unrepresented.

"*Rhode Island* is the delinquent state," commented the Massachusetts *Centinel*, "but . . . this is a circumstance far *more joyous than grievous*; for . . . her deputation, if . . . they should have been *birds of feather* with the majority of her present administration, must have been the cause of much mortification to the illustrious characters who now compose that assembly [the Convention]."

The New Englanders ranged from grave, dignified scholars and judges like Dr. William Johnson and Oliver Ellsworth (Connecticut), to an attractive young lawyer, Rufus King (Massachusetts) and an eccentric Roger Sherman. Roger Sherman, shaped like a corkscrew and "cunning as the Devil," had risen from a shoemaker's to a judge's bench in Connecticut. As a group they were unpredictable. Spare Elbridge Gerry, the Marblehead tycoon, was typical in wavering between a nationalist and an antinationalist position. He seemed to be always anxiously rubbing his nose, trying to make up his mind.

Young William Pierce, a delegate from Georgia, wrote descriptions of his colleagues. (He was not completely accurate when he gave their ages.) The following selection is from his sketches of the New Englanders (from Max Farrand, ed., *The Records of the Federal Convention of 1787*, III).

Mr. Sherman exhibits the oddest shaped character I ever remember to have met with. He is awkward, un-meaning, and unaccountably strange in his manner. But in his train of thinking there is something regular, deep and comprehensive; yet the oddity of his address, the vulgarisms that accompany his public speaking, and that strange New England cant which runs through his public as well as his private speaking make everything that is connected with him grotesque and laughable;—and yet he deserves infinite praise,—no Man has a better Heart or a clearer Head. If he cannot embellish he can furnish thoughts that are wise and useful.

He is an able politician, and extremely artful in accomplishing any particular object;—it is remarked that he seldom fails. I am told he sits on the Bench in Connecticut, and is very correct in the discharge of his Judicial functions. In the early part of his life he was a Shoe-maker;—but despising the lowness of his condition, he turned Almanack maker, and so progressed upwards to a Judge. . . . He is about 60.

Mr. King is a Man much distinguished for his eloquence and great parliamentary talents. . . . This Gentleman is about thirty three years of age, about five feet ten Inches high, well formed, an handsome face, with a strong expressive Eye, and a sweet high toned voice. In his public speaking there is something peculiarly strong and rich in his expression, clear, and convincing in his arguments. . . . He may with propriety be ranked among the Luminaries of the present Age.

Mr. Gorham is a Merchant in Boston, high in reputation, and much in esteem of his Country-men. He is a Man of very good sense, but not much improved in his education. He is eloquent and easy in public debate, but has nothing fashionable or elegant in his style. . . . Mr. Gorham is about 46 years of age, rather lusty, and has an agreeable and pleasing manner.

Mr. Gerry's character is marked for integrity and perseverance. He is a hesitating and laborious speaker;—possesses a great degree of confidence and goes extensively into all subjects. . . . Mr. Gerry is very much of a Gentleman in his principles and manners;—he has been engaged in the mercantile line and is a Man of property. He is about 37 years of age.

NATIONALISTS OF THE MIDDLE STATES

In the prosperous Middle Atlantic States were many lawyers and businessmen who wanted a stable government. This section sent a number of outstanding nationalists to the Convention. There were just three delegates from New York, but eight from Pennsylvania and five each from New Jersey, Delaware, and Maryland.

Pennsylvania's Benjamin Franklin, Robert Morris, bespectacled James Wilson, and irrepressible Gouverneur Morris, the "Tall Boy" who had lost a leg, made a strong team. They were supported by Alexander Hamilton of New York and John Dickinson of Delaware. True, New York also sent two antinationalist delegates who would outvote the brilliant Hamilton; and Maryland was divided, with its red-faced attorney general Luther Martin raging against any attempt to lessen the sovereignty of the Old Line State. But both New Jersey and Delaware would, if their statehood were respected, aid Pennsylvania's powerful group.

So Benjamin Franklin could have renewed hopes for a stronger Union—although he was now so weak that he would have to be carried to the State House each morning in a sedan chair, by four husky prisoners from the Walnut Street jail.

The following selection, describing leading delegates from the Middle States, is from William Pierce's sketches (from Max Farrand, ed., *The Records of the Federal Convention of 1787*, III).

Colo. Hamilton is deservedly celebrated for his talents. He is a practitioner of the Law, and reputed to be a finished Scholar. To a clear and strong judgment he unites the ornaments of fancy, and whilst he is able, convincing, and engaging in his eloquence the Heart and Head sympathize in approving him. Yet there is something too feeble in his voice to be equal to the strains of oratory;—it is my opinion that he is rather a convincing Speaker, that [than] a blazing Orator.

Colo. Hamilton requires time to think,—he enquires into every part of his subject with the searchings of philosophy, and when he comes forward he comes highly charged with interesting matter, there is no skimming over the surface of a subject with him, he must sink to the bottom to see what foundation it rests on. . . . His eloquence is not so diffusive as to trifle with the senses, but he rambles just enough to strike and keep up the attention.

He is about 33 years old, of small stature, and lean. His manners are tinctured with stiffness, and sometimes with a degree of vanity that is highly disagreeable.

Dr. Franklin is well known to be the greatest philosopher of the present age;—all the operations of nature he seems to understand,—the very heavens obey him, and the Clouds yield up their Lightning to be imprisoned in his rod. But what claim he has to the politician, posterity must determine. It is certain that he does not shine much in public Council,—he is no Speaker, nor does he seem to let politics engage his attention.

He is, however, a most extraordinary Man and tells a story in a style more engaging than anything I ever heard. . . . He is 82 years old, and possesses an activity of mind equal to a youth of 25 years of age.

Mr. Wilson ranks among the foremost in legal and political knowledge. . . . He is well acquainted with Man, and understands all the passions that influence him. Government seems to have been his peculiar Study, all the political institutions of the World he knows in detail, and can trace the causes and effects of every revolution from the earliest stages of the Grecian commonwealth down to the present time. No man is more clear, copious, and comprehensive than Mr. Wilson, yet he is no great Orator. He draws the attention not by the charm of his eloquence, but by the force of his reasoning. He is about 45 years old.

Mr. Gouverneur Morris is one of those Genius's in whom every species of talents combine to render him conspicuous and flourishing in public debate:—He winds through all the mazes of rhetoric, and throws around him such a glare that he charms, captivates, and leads away the senses of all who hear him. . . . But with all these powers he is fickle and inconstant,

—never pursuing one train of thinking,—nor ever regular.

He has gone through a very extensive course of reading, and is acquainted with all the sciences. No Man has more wit,—nor can any one engage the attention more than Mr. Morris. He was bred to the Law, but I am told he disliked the profession, and turned merchant. He is engaged in some great mercantile matters with his namesake Mr. Robt. Morris.

This Gentleman is about 38 years old, he has been unfortunate in losing one of his Legs, and getting all the flesh taken off his right arm by a scald, when a youth.

Mr. Paterson is one of those . . . Men whose powers break in upon you, and create wonder and astonishment. He is a Man of great modesty, with looks that bespeak talents of no great extent—but he is a Classic, a Lawyer, and an Orator. . . . He . . . never speaks but when he understands his subject well. This Gentleman is about 34 years of age, of a very low stature.

Mr. Dickinson has been famed through all America, for his Farmers Letters; he is a Scholar, and said to be a Man of very extensive information. . . . I had often heard that he was a great Orator, but I found him an indifferent Speaker. With an affected air of wisdom he labors to produce a trifle,—his language is irregular and incorrect,—his flourishes (for he sometimes attempts them), are like expiring flames, they just shew themselves and go out. . . .

He is, however, a good writer and will ever be considered one of the most important characters in the United States. He is about 55 years old, and was bred a Quaker.

John Dickinson's *Letters from an American Farmer* (1767–68) had gained him fame as an early defender of American liberties. Dickinson, like Franklin, was a kind of distinguished elder statesman at the Convention.

> Mr. [Luther] Martin was educated for the Bar, and is Attorney general for the State of Maryland. This Gentleman possesses a good deal of information, but he has a very bad delivery, and so extremely prolix, that he never speaks without tiring the patience of all who hear him. He is about 34 years of age.

SOUTHERN ARISTOCRATS

The South was a region unto itself. It had great tidewater plantations, worked by hundreds of black slaves; rolling Piedmont backwoods where yeomen had carved their small farms out of the forest; and wide southwestern marshes, ranged by hostile Indians.

Because of the plantations and the Indians, the South was nationalist-minded. The wealthy gentry, or "nabobs" as Northerners called them, wanted efficient government and a sound currency to protect their property. The yeomen, who took little interest in the doings of a distant Congress, nevertheless might need help from the central government against the red men whose lands they coveted.

Also, the Southern aristocrats who controlled local politics were trained in the law, and some were well read in Greek and Latin political treatises. They were eager to erect a strong republic that Europe would respect. George Washington, a practical man from his earliest hunting and surveying days, had long urged that the Confederation be strengthened. James "Jemmy" Madison —"no bigger than half a piece of soap," according to a contemporary—was a keen politician and deep student of ancient constitutions.

Likewise nationalist-minded were Madison's colleagues from Virginia, including George Mason, the fiercely independent liberal, and handsome, dark-haired Governor Edmund Randolph; also, Hugh Williamson of North Carolina and the two Pinckneys and John Rutledge of South Carolina. Fortunately for the nationalists Patrick Henry, a fiery republican champion of local government, stayed home. Henry said he "smelt a rat."

One other distinguished absentee was Thomas Jefferson. Like John Adams, ambassador to Britain, he was kept overseas by his assignment as diplomat. But Jefferson, ambassador to France, kept in close touch with his younger disciple James Madison.

Red-haired "Long Tom" with his serious blue-gray eyes scanned scores of treatises on constitutions, then bundled them up and sent them to "Jemmy." One shipment included a thirty-seven-volume encyclopedia! Madison was soon the most formidable champion of nationalist ideas that any antinationalist might encounter.

Virginia's seven-man delegation was the largest from the South; South Carolina sent four planter-lawyer aristocrats, North Carolina five solid citizens, and Georgia four.

The following selection, describing some of the Southern delegates, is from William Pierce's sketches (from Max Farrand, ed., *The Records of the Federal Convention of 1787*, III).

Genl. Washington is well known as the Commander in chief of the late American Army. Having conducted these states to independence and peace, he now appears to assist in framing a Government to make the People happy. Like Gustavus Vasa, he may be said to be the deliverer of his Country;—like Peter the great he appears as the politician and the States-man; and like Cincinnatus he returned to his farm perfectly contented with being only a plain Citizen, after enjoying the highest honor of the Confederacy,—and now only seeks for the approbation of his Country-men by being virtuous and useful.

The General was conducted to the Chair as President of the Convention by the unanimous voice of its Members. He is in the 52d. year of his age.

Mr. Madison is a character who has long been in public life; and what is very remarkable every Person seems to acknowledge his greatness. He blends together the profound politician, with the Scholar. In the management of every great question he evidently took the lead in the Convention, and tho' he cannot be called an Orator, he is a most agreeable, eloquent, and convincing Speaker. . . . He always comes forward the best informed Man of any point in debate. The affairs of the United States, he perhaps, has the most correct knowledge of, of any Man in the Union.

Mr. Madison is about 37 years of age, a Gentleman of great modesty,—with a remarkable sweet temper. He is easy and unreserved among his acquaintance, and has a most agreeable style of conversation.

Mr. Mason is a Gentleman of remarkable strong powers, and possesses a clear and copious understanding. He is able and convincing in debate, steady and firm in his principles, and undoubtedly one of the best politicians in America. Mr. Mason is about 60 years old, with a fine strong constitution.

Mr. Randolph is Governor of Virginia,—a young Gentleman in whom unite all the accomplishments of the Scholar, and the States-man. He came forward with the . . . first principles, on which the Convention acted, and he supported them with a force of eloquence and reasoning that did him great honor. He has a most harmonious voice, a fine person and striking manners. Mr. Randolph is about 32 years of age.

Mr. Charles Pinckney is a young Gentleman of the most promising talents. He is, altho' only 24 ys. of age, in possession of a very great variety of knowledge. Government, Law, History and Philosophy are his favorite studies. . . . He speaks with great neatness and perspicuity, and treats every subject . . . fully, without running into prolixity.

ON STAGE—RUMORS AND STRATAGEMS

The Convention was scheduled to open Monday, May 14. But, as George Washington dryly noted in his diary, "it was found that two States only were represented, viz., Virginia and Pennsylvania." The Pennsylvanians were there because most of them "lived within shouting distance" of the State House; the Virginians had been hurried along by James Madison. Bad weather and the habit of procrastinating delayed the other politicians for another eleven days, or longer.

The next few days were damp; there was still no quorum. On Wednesday a "cask was broached" at Benjamin Franklin's house. The "contents met with the most cordial reception," said Franklin. He described his guests as "what the French call *une assemblée des notables* . . .

some of the principal people from the several States of our confederation."

Franklin himself was described by a visitor as "a short, fat . . . old man in a plain Quaker dress, bald pate and short white locks." The world-famous scientist and diplomat joked about his eighty-one years: "I have lived long enough to intrude myself on posterity."

While waiting, the Virginians decided not to waste their time. At the Indian Queen and other inns they held strategy sessions. In the following paragraphs George Mason tells how the Virginians sized up the situation and their fellow delegates. The selection is from George Mason's letter to his son, May 20, 1787 (from Max Farrand, ed., *The Records of the Federal Convention of 1787*, III).

Philadelphia, May 20th, 1787

. . . The Virginia deputies . . . meet and confer together two or three hours every day. . . . I have reason to hope there will be greater unanimity and less opposition, except from the little States, than was at first apprehended.

The most prevalent idea in the principal States seems to be a total alteration of the present federal system, and substituting a great national council or parliament, consisting of two branches of the legislature, founded upon the principles of equal proportionate representation, with full legislative powers upon all the subjects of the Union; and an executive: and to make the several State legislatures subordinate to the national. . . .

It is easy to foresee that there will be much difficulty in organizing a government upon this great scale . . . yet with a proper degree of coolness, liberality and candor . . . I doubt not but it may be effected. There are . . . some very eccentric opinions upon this great subject; and what is a very extraordinary phenomenon, we are likely to find the republicans [nationalists], on this occasion, issue from the Southern and Middle States, and the anti-republicans [antinationalists] from the Eastern [New England]. . . . Men disappointed in expectations too . . . sanguinely formed . . . are very apt to run into the opposite extreme; and the people of the Eastern States [New England], setting out with more republican principles [than the South and Middle States], have consequently been more disappointed than we have been.

We found travelling very expensive—from eight to nine dollars per day. In this city the living is cheap. We are at the old *Indian Queen* in Fourth Street, where we are very well accommodated, have a good room to ourselves, and are charged only twenty-five Pennsylvania currency per day.

Shays' Rebellion in Massachusetts and Rhode Island's spree of printing inflationary paper money probably accounted for the disillusionment of some New Englanders with "republican principles." They came to the Convention less optimistic than the energetic Middle and Southern states' delegates.

One Virginian, however, elegant Colonel William Grayson, held a different view from Mason's. This antinationalist member of Congress wrote from New York, "I hardly think much good can come of it [the Constitutional Convention]." The following selection is from Grayson's letter to James Monroe, May 29, 1787 (from Max Farrand, ed., *The Records of the Federal Convention of 1787,* III).

New York May 29th. 1787

. . . What will be the result of their meeting [the Constitutional Convention] I cannot with any cer-

tainty determine, but I hardly think much good can
come of it: the people of America don't appear to me
to be ripe for any great innovations. . . . The weight
of Genl. Washington . . . is very great in America,
but I hardly think it is sufficient to induce the people
to pay money or part with power.

The delegates from the Eastwd. [New England]
are for a very strong government . . . but I don't learn
that the people are with them, on the contrary in
Massachusetts they think that government too strong
& are about rebelling again, for the purpose of making it more democratical: In Connecticut they have
rejected the requisition [Congress' request for
money] for the present year. . . . Rhode Island has
refused to send members—the cry there is for a good
government after they have paid their debts in de-
preciated paper. . . .

New Hampshire has not paid a shilling, since
peace, & does not ever mean to pay one to all eter-
nity:—if it was attempted to tax the people for the
domestic [national] debt 500 Shays would arise in a
fortnight.—In New York they pay well because they
can do it by plundering New Jersey & Connecticut. . . .
Pennsylvania will join provided you let the sessions
of the Executive of America be fixed in Philada. &
give her other advantages in trade. . . . On the southern States . . . I think they will be . . . as little disposed to part with efficient power as any in the
Union.

On a rainy Friday, May 25, the gavel of the temporary
chairman fell in the high-ceilinged east room of the State
House. Twenty-nine gentlemen broke off their conversations. A few standing by the marble-faced twin fireplaces
seated themselves at the tables with the others. They rep-

resented seven states—a quorum at last. Robert Morris, the hearty, thick-necked "Financier," arose.

"Mr. Chairman," he said, "by the instruction and in behalf of the deputation of Pennsylvania I nominate General Washington for president of the Convention."

"I second the motion, sir," said John Rutledge of South Carolina. "I am confident that this choice will be unanimous."

The "Ayes" that rang out when the vote was taken justified John Rutledge's confidence. He and Robert Morris escorted George Washington to the raised platform between the fireplaces at the east end.

George Washington, six feet four inches tall, wore his hair powdered and brushed straight back. His direct blue eyes could be calm or icy. For the next four months he would preside over the assembly with awe-inspiring dignity.

So the Convention began. In the end, fifty-five delegates would present the views of twelve of the thirteen states. Of these delegates, forty-two had served in Congress; thirty had fought in the Revolution; fifty-two had held office. They were planters, lawyers, merchants, and politicians—twenty-six with college or university study behind them, many others trained in the law or privately educated.

Black slaves, however, were not represented, nor were the debtor backwoodsmen, hoeing amid charred stumps on their newly cleared lands.

Could these fifty-five men of the middle and upper classes make a constitution that went beyond safeguarding their own property? Perhaps the chief hope that they might lay in the broad education of some of them. As the Convention opened, James Madison, Alexander Hamilton, and others were reviewing European history—seeking ideas in the political classics of ancient and modern times.

GUIDELINES
FROM HISTORY

I have but one lamp by which my feet are guided, and that is the lamp of experience. I know of no way of judging the future but by the past.

—Patrick Henry

ATHENS POINTS THE WAY

The first to experiment with government "by the people, for the people" were the ancient Greeks. Twenty-five hundred years ago, each small, sunlit Greek city perched on its hill by some landlocked cove of the blue Aegean Sea had its own citadel, marketplace, and lawcourts. Each was a mini-nation—a "city-state," complete and independent. And each devised its own form of government, sometimes a kingship, sometimes government by the rich (an oligarchy), but often government by the people—a democracy.

The Greeks were curious about everything. They were always asking questions. Why? How? For what purpose? They asked these questions about governments. One famous Greek thinker, whom later ages would know simply as the Philosopher, made a collection of 158 constitutions of Greek cities. This thinker, Aristotle, then wrote a treatise which expressed some basic ideas.

The ideas in Aristotle's *Politics* were adopted by the English Whigs, a party representing the middle class. From these seventeenth- and eighteenth-century English Whigs the Americans borrowed the same ideas. They packed them, as well as their clothes, for the trip to Philadelphia.

What were these basic ideas about government?

One was that there should be a constitution for any government—that is, a regular plan based on customs that had grown up, about how the different positions were to be filled. Another was that everyone, including the rulers, should obey the law; there should be a government of laws, not of men. A third was that the people were the real boss; they had the right to choose their lawmakers. These lawmakers, however, would have only certain, specified, *limited* powers.

Aristotle, who wrote down these thoughts, was not only an outstanding teacher, but a man with firsthand experience of governments himself. He was a neatly dressed man with firm lips and intent eyes that didn't miss anything that went on. "Observation shows us—" these are the words with which he began his *Politics*. And he observed, not only in Athens, the most cultured city of Greece, but also in Macedon, the center of power. There he had been the tutor of Alexander the Great, the future world conqueror. He had married the adopted daughter of another ruler, Hermias, in Asia Minor.

Toward the end of his life, when he was the head of what we would call a university, he wrote his *Politics*. His school, the Lyceum, was located in a green grove on the outskirts of Athens. It had small buildings and shady covered walks beside the rippling stream Ilissus. Aristotle discussed his ideas about government with his students as they strolled down the walks; hence they were called *peripatetic* ("walking") philosophers.

Aristotle was the philosopher of moderation or the golden mean. Therefore, he concluded that a government dominated by neither the rich nor the poor but by the average people in between would be best. But he also expressed his belief in the good judgment of the people as a whole. These two ideas are stated in the following selection, from Aristotle's *Politics*, composed 335–322 B.C. (from *The Politics of Aristotle*, tr. by Ernest Barker).

That the people at large should be sovereign rather than the few best would appear to be defensible. . . . There is this to be said for the Many. Each of them by himself may not be of a good quality; but when they all come together it is possible that they may surpass . . . the quality of the few best.

Feasts to which many contribute may excel those provided at one man's expense. In the same way, when there are many who contribute to the process of deliberation, each can bring his share of goodness and moral prudence; and when all meet together the people may thus become something in the nature of a single person, who—as he has many feet, many hands, and many senses—may also have many qualities of character and intelligence. This is the reason why the Many are also better judges than the few of music and the writings of poets: some appreciate one part, some another, and all together appreciate all. . . .

It would thus seem possible to solve . . . both the problem raised in the previous chapter "What body of *persons* should be sovereign?" and the further problem . . . "What are the *matters* over which freemen, or the general body of citizens—men of the sort who neither have wealth nor can make any claim on the ground of goodness—should properly exercise sovereignty?"

It may be argued, from one point of view, that it is dangerous for men of this sort to share in the highest offices, as injustice may lead them into wrongdoing, and thoughtlessness into error. But it may also be argued, from another point of view, that there is serious risk in not letting them have *some* share in the enjoyment of power; for a state with a body of disfranchised citizens who are numerous and poor must necessarily be a state which is full of enemies.

The alternative left is to let them share in the deliberative and judicial functions; and we thus find Solon [famous Athenian lawgiver], and some of the other legislators, giving the people the two general functions of electing the magistrates to office and of calling them to account at the end of their tenure of office, but *not* the right of holding office themselves in their individual capacity. There is wisdom in such a policy. When they all meet together, the people display a good enough gift of perception, and combined with the better class they are of service to the state . . . but each of them is imperfect in the judgments he forms by himself. . . .

[However, for all forms of government] rightly constituted laws should be the final sovereign; and personal rule, whether it be exercised by a single person or a body of persons, should be sovereign only in those matters on which law is unable, owing to the difficulty of framing general rules for all contingencies, to make an exact pronouncement.

We have now to consider what is the best constitution and the best way of life for the *majority* of states and men. . . .

In all states there may be distinguished three parts, or classes, of the citizen-body—the very rich; the very poor; and the middle class which forms the mean. Now it is admitted, as a general principle, that moderation and the mean are always best. We may therefore conclude that in the ownership of all gifts of fortune a middle condition will be the best.

Men who are in this condition are the most ready to listen to reason. Those who belong to either extreme—the over-handsome, the over-strong, the over-noble, the over-wealthy; or at the opposite end the over-poor, the over-weak, the utterly ignoble—find it hard to follow the lead of reason. Men in the first class tend more to violence and serious crime; men in the second tend too much to roguery and petty offences. . . . It must also be added that those who enjoy too many advantages . . . are both unwilling to obey and ignorant how to obey. This is a defect which appears in them from the first, during childhood and in home-life; nurtured in luxury, they never acquire a habit of discipline, even in the matter of lessons. But . . . those who suffer from the opposite extreme of a lack of advantages . . . are far too mean and poor-spirited.

We have thus, on the one hand, people who are ignorant how to rule and only know how to obey . . . and, on the other hand, people who are ignorant how to obey any sort of authority and only know how to rule. . . . The result is a state, not of freemen, but only of slaves and masters: a state of envy on the one side and on the other contempt. Nothing could be further removed from the spirit of friendship or the temper of a political community. . . .

A state aims at being, as far as it can be, a society composed of equals and peers who, as such, can be friends and associates; and the middle class, more than any other, has this sort of composition. It follows that a state which is based on the middle class is bound to be the best constituted. . . . The middle classes . . . do not, like the poor, covet the goods of others; nor do others covet their possessions, as the poor covet those of the rich. . . .

[Thus] it is clear that the middle type of constitution is best for the *majority* of states. It is the one type free from faction; where the middle class is large, there is least likelihood of faction and dissension among the citizens. Large states are generally more free from faction just because they have a large middle class. In small states, on the other hand, it is easy for the whole population to be divided into only two classes; nothing is left in the middle, and all—or almost all—are either poor or rich.

The reason why democracies are generally more

secure and more permanent than oligarchies is the character of their middle class, which is more numerous, and is allowed a larger share in the government, than it is in oligarchies. Where democracies have no middle class, and the poor are greatly superior in numbers, trouble ensues, and they are speedily ruined.

CHAMPION OF THE MIDDLE CLASS

The delegates at Philadelphia liked the way the Greeks emphasized having a constitution. They also approved of Aristotle's golden mean between government by the rich and an extreme democracy. In the writings of an Englishman of the middle class, John Locke, they found further support for these ideas.

John Locke was a rather timid professor and physician who taught at Oxford University in the seventeenth century. He was a bachelor who suffered from asthma and was happiest in his study, surrounded by hundreds of golden, calfskin-bound books.

But Locke came out of his study to fight for the independent beliefs of his Puritan forefathers. He gave advice and wrote papers for a leading Whig politician, Lord Shaftesbury, who opposed the Stuart kings then ruling England. As a result, the royalist party had Locke dismissed from his position at Oxford, and he had to go into exile in Holland. No wonder he wrote two treatises on toleration! He believed not only in freedom in the choice of one's religion, but in freedom of speech in general.

In 1688, the Glorious Revolution drove James II, the last Stuart king, from the English throne. The Whigs brought in their candidate from the Netherlands, William of Orange. The real power in the English government passed over to the middle-class Parliament. And John Locke, with his asthma and his keen mind, returned to England.

The very next year, 1689, he published his *Two Treatises of Government*. This work not only justified the Glorious Revolution, but also voiced progressive, even revolutionary, ideas. It established Locke as the champion of the middle class and of the rights of the individual.

For example, the royalists had argued that kings were appointed by God; it would be a sin to disobey them. Kings thus ruled by divine right. But Locke, the descendant of the sturdy Puritans and a believer in reason, said no. There was no divine power behind any government. Government was simply a rational arrangement made by men to protect their lives and their property.

It was a "compact"—that is, a contract—made between the people and those they chose to rule them. Individuals living in a "state of nature," roaming the woods like American Indians, agreed to come together and form a state and let the state establish law and order. But if the government they set up became corrupt or tyrannous, they had the right to revolt, to overthrow it and establish another.

Americans had appealed to John Locke's ideas in 1776, when they rebelled against Britain. He was known as "America's philosopher." He had also stated that men, as rational beings, are born "free" and "equal," and Thomas Jefferson had borrowed these famous words for the Declaration of Independence. Now, eleven years later as the American constitution makers gathered, Locke's ideas were almost like proverbs for them. They would be especially influenced by his idea of government as a compact and by his strong bourgeois emphasis on protecting private property.

The following selection, stating several of Locke's leading ideas, is from his *Two Treatises of Government* (*1689*).

Men being . . . by Nature, all free, equal and independent, no one can be put out of this Estate, and subjected to the Political Power of another, without his own *Consent*. The only way whereby any one divests himself of his Natural Liberty, and *puts on the bonds of Civil Society* is by agreeing with other Men to join and unite into a Community, for their comfortable, safe, and peaceable living one amongst another, in a secure Enjoyment of their Properties, and a greater Security against any that are not of it. . . . When any number of Men have so *consented to make one Community* or Government, they are thereby presently incorporated, and make *one Body Politic*, wherein the *Majority* have a Right to act and conclude the rest. . . .

And thus every Man, by consenting with others to make one Body Politic under one Government, puts himself under an Obligation to every one of that Society, to submit to the determination of the *majority* and to be concluded by it; or else this *original Compact*, whereby he with others incorporates into *one Society*, would signify nothing, and be no Compact, if he be left free, and under no other ties than he was in before in the State of Nature. . . .

Whosoever therefore out of a state of Nature unite into a *Community*, must be understood to give up all the power, necessary to the ends for which they unite into Society, to the *majority* of the Community.

The Reason why Men enter into Society, is the preservation of their Property. . . . Since it can never be supposed to be the Will of the Society, that the Legislative should have a Power to destroy that, which every one designs to secure, by entering into Society, and for which the People submitted themselves to the Legislators of their own making; whenever the *Legislators endeavour to take away, and destroy the Property of the People,* or to reduce them to Slavery under Arbitrary Power, they put themselves into a state of War with the People, who are thereupon absolved from any farther Obedience. . . .

Whensoever therefore the *Legislative* shall . . . *endeavour to grasp* themselves, *or put into the hands of any other an Absolute Power* over the Lives, Liberties, and Estates of the People; By this breach of Trust they *forfeit the Power*, the People had put into their hands . . . and it devolves [returns] to the People, who have a Right to resume their original Liberty, and by the Establishment of a new Legislative . . . provide for their own Safety and Security.

WHAT IS POLITICAL FREEDOM?

In eighteenth-century Europe police brutality and the disregard of the individual's rights were common. A press gang might seize you illegally in some tavern and enroll you in the Navy for years to come. A powerful man at court might have you unjustly discharged from your position and left to starve. Americans wanted to guard against these injustices of the Old World. But how?

Among the books they searched for ideas was one by a Frenchman, the Baron de Montesquieu's *Spirit of Laws* (1748). In this work many delegates found a definition of political liberty that they liked. Liberty is *not* the freedom to do anything you wish to, because if everyone had that freedom, you would find your life very uncomfortable and very unfree! Liberty is, instead, "a right of doing whatever the laws permit"—*i.e.*, it is equal protection under the law.

The delegates also found in Montesquieu's book an explanation and defense of the Anglo-Saxon system of government they were familiar with, the separation of powers. Montesquieu convinced them that this separation of powers offered the best protection against tyrannical officials.

In brief, Montesquieu observed that men will always seek power and be corrupted by it. Therefore, he recommended dividing up the power of government so that no one man or group of men would have too much.

Let the men who make the laws (the legislators) be different from those who enforce the laws (the executive). And let those who judge cases (the judiciary) be still another group of men. Then some powerful executive official could not get a man unjustly discharged from his position; an independent judge would say "Just a minute!" and restore the man to his post. To avoid injustice, the three branches of government—our Congress, President, and Supreme Court—should be as distinct as the three leaves of a clover!

Baron de Montesquieu was a wise and witty nobleman who favored moderate reforms in the eighteenth-century French monarchy. After producing a clever satire on the follies of his country, *The Persian Letters* (1721), he completed his masterpiece, *The Spirit of Laws* (1748). *The Spirit of Laws* was the first great work of the French *philosophes*, or rationalists—a comparative study of the governments and customs of many peoples.

Two other ideas of Montesquieu's which Americans frequently debated were that a republic would not last if it were too large and that the citizens of a republic had to be honest to make that form of government work. The Philadelphia delegates had an answer to the first idea (see pg. 145), but they fervently agreed with the second.

The following selection, presenting several of these ideas, is from Montesquieu's *Spirit of Laws* (tr. by Thomas Nugent, 1873).

Different Significations of the Word "Liberty"

There is no word that admits of more various significations . . . than that of *Liberty*. Some have taken it for a facility of deposing a person on whom they had conferred a tyrannical authority; others for the power of choosing a superior whom they are obliged to obey; others for the right of bearing arms, and of being thereby enabled to use violence; others, in fine, for the privilege of being governed by a native of their own country, or by their own laws.

A certain nation [Russia], for a long time thought liberty consisted in the privilege of wearing a long beard. Some have annexed this name to one form of government exclusive of others: those who had a republican taste, applied it to this species of polity; those who liked a monarchical state, gave it to monarchy.

Thus they have all applied the name of *liberty* to the government most suitable to their own customs and inclinations; and as in republics the people have not so constant and so present a view of the causes of their misery, and as the magistrates seem to act only in conformity to the laws, hence liberty is generally said to reside in republics, and to be banished from monarchies. In fine, as in democracies the people seem to act almost as they please; this sort of government has been deemed the most free; and the power of the people has been confounded with their liberty.

In What Liberty Consists

It is true, that in democracies the people seem to act as they please; but political liberty does not consist in an unlimited freedom. In governments, that is, in societies directed by laws, liberty can consist only in the power of doing what we ought to will, and in not being constrained to do what we ought not to will.

We must have continually present to our minds the difference between independence and liberty. Liberty is a right of doing whatever the laws permit; and if a citizen could do what they forbid, he would be no longer possessed of liberty, because all his fellow-citizens would have the same power.

Of the End or View of different Governments

Though all governments have the same general end, which is that of preservation, yet each has another particular object. Increase of dominion was the object of Rome; war, that of Sparta; religion, that of the Jewish laws; commerce, that of Marseilles; public tranquillity, that of the laws of China; navigation, that of the laws of Rhodes; natural liberty, that of the policy of the Savages. . . .

One nation there is also in the world, that has for the direct end of its constitution, political liberty. [That nation is England.] We shall presently examine the principles on which this liberty is founded; if they are sound, liberty will appear in its highest perfection. . . .

Of the Constitution of England

. . . In every government there are three sorts of power: the legislative; the executive . . . ; [and] the judiciary power.

When the legislative and executive powers are united in the same person, or in the same body of magistrates, there can be no liberty; because apprehensions may arise, lest the same monarch or senate should enact tyrannical laws, to execute them in a tyrannical manner.

Again, there is no liberty if the judiciary power be not separated from the legislative and executive. Were it joined with the legislative, the life and liberty of the subject would be exposed to arbitrary control; for the judge would be then the legislator. Were it joined to the executive power, the judge might behave with violence and oppression. . . .

In a country of liberty . . . the legislative power should reside in the whole body of the people. But since this is impossible in large states, and in small ones is subject to many inconveniences, it is fit the people should transact by their representatives, what they cannot transact by themselves.

The inhabitants of a particular town are much better acquainted with its wants and interests, than with those of other places; and are better judges of the capacity of their neighbours, than of that of the rest of their countrymen. The members, therefore, of the legislature should not be chosen from the general body of the nation; but it is proper that in every considerable place, a representative should be elected by the inhabitants. . . .

The legislative power is [therefore] committed to

the body of the nobles, and to that which represents the people, each having their assemblies and deliberations apart, each their separate views and interests. . . .

The executive power ought to be in the hands of a monarch, because this branch of government, having need of dispatch, is better administered by one than by many: on the other hand, whatever depends on the legislative power, is oftentimes better regulated by many than by a single person. . . .

The executive power . . . ought to have a share in the legislature by the power of rejecting [vetoing], otherwise it would soon be stripped of its prerogative. . . .

Here then is the fundamental constitution of the government we are treating of. The legislative body being composed of two parts, they check one another by the mutual privilege of rejecting. They are both restrained by the executive power, as the executive is by the legislative.

On the Principle of Democracy

There is no great share of probity [honesty] necessary to support a monarchical or despotic government. The force of laws in one, and the prince's arm in the other, are sufficient to direct and maintain the whole. But in a popular state, one spring more is necessary, namely, *virtue*. . . .

When virtue is banished, ambition invades the minds of those who are disposed to receive it, and avarice possesses the whole community. The objects of their desires are changed; what they were fond of before, is become indifferent; they were free, while under the restraint of laws, but they would fain now be free to act against law; and as each citizen is like a slave who has run away from his master, what was a maxim of equity [justice], he calls rigour; what was a rule of action, he styles constraint. . . . The members of the commonwealth riot on the public spoils, and its strength is only the power of a few, and the licentiousness of many.

CONFRONTATIONS
AND WALKOUTS

A contest for power, not for liberty.
—ALEXANDER HAMILTON

A REPORTER AT THE CONVENTION

Twenty-nine delegates, their ideas drawn from political classics as well as their own experience, met on a gray May 25 for their first session. They did not know that there was a reporter in their midst. They elected Major William Jackson as their official secretary—but their unofficial secretary and future historian was James Madison.

Madison chose a table at the front, spread out paper and pens, and prepared to watch—and listen. Just thirty-six, this small, alert scholar, who usually wore black and walked with a quick, bouncing step, was at the height of his powers. None of the crucial struggles of the Convention would escape him. All would be mirrored in the clear prose of his *Debates in the Federal Convention of 1787*.

The following selection, in which Madison tells why he decided to appoint himself reporter, is from the Preface to his *Debates in the Federal Convention of 1787* (first published by the State Department, 1900).

The curiosity I had felt during my researches into the History of the most distinguished Confederacies, particularly those of antiquity, and the deficiency I found in the means of satisfying it . . . determined me to preserve as far as I could an exact account of what might pass in the Convention. . . . Nor was I unaware of the value of such a contribution to . . . the History of a Constitution on which would be staked the happiness of a people great even in its infancy, and possibly the cause of Liberty throughout the world.

In pursuance of the task I had assumed I chose a seat in front of the presiding member, with the other members on my right & left hands. In this favorable position for hearing all that passed, I noted in terms legible & in abbreviations & marks intelligible to myself what was read from the Chair or spoken by the members; and losing not a moment unnecessarily between the adjournment & reassembling of the Convention I was enabled to write my daily notes. . . .

In the labour & correctness of doing this, I was not a little aided by practice & by a familiarity with the style and the train of observation & reasoning which characterized the principal speakers. It happened, also that I was not absent a single day, nor more than a casual fraction of an hour in any day, so that I could not have lost a single speech, unless a very short one.

SKETCH FOR A NATION

Any meeting must have rules if it is not to end in disorder. The delegates were all familiar with parliamentary procedure—motions, seconds, adjournments, etc. But they now adopted two additional rules: that each state would have one vote (as under the Articles of Confederation) and that they would keep their discussions secret until the Convention ended.

They would not publicize their conflicts and thus perhaps make them worse. Surprisingly, there were no leaks. A cousin of Madison's, a college president, tried to pump him about what was happening but learned nothing. "If you cannot tell us what you are doing," said this scholar in exasperation, "you might at least give us some information of what you are *not* doing!"

Things *were* happening, though. Four days after the Convention opened, Edmund Randolph presented the Virginia Plan. This was an outline not for a league or confederation, but for a nation. It provided for a Congress ("National Legislature") and a President which would be supreme over the states. It was largely the work of the behind-the-scenes manager of the Convention, "Jemmy" Madison.

The Convention decided to discuss the Virginia Plan as a committee of the whole. Any voting would not count officially. The delegates could brainstorm about the plan, change their minds, take votes over, until they reached a consensus. But one of the first votes taken, although it did not count officially, was never reversed. This was a vote, 6–1, to provide for a "*national* government."

One other plan was presented at this time, but was never discussed. It was that of young Charles Pinckney, who later claimed to have contributed so much to the Constitution that fellow South Carolinians nicknamed him "Constitution Charlie."

The following selection is from the Virginia Plan, as revised after two weeks' discussion in the Convention. It is from James Madison's *Debates in the Federal Convention of 1787* (first published 1900).

June 13

1. Resolved that . . . a National Government ought to be established, consisting of a supreme Legislative, Executive & Judiciary.

2. Resolved that the National Legislature ought to consist of two branches.

3. Resolved that the members of the first branch of the National Legislature ought to be elected by

the people of the several States for the term of three years. . . .

4. Resolved that the members of the second branch of the National Legislature ought to be chosen by the individual [State] Legislatures . . . for . . . seven years. . . .

6. Resolved that the National Legislature ought to be empowered to . . . negative all laws passed by the several States contravening . . . the articles of Union, or any treaties subsisting under the authority of the Union.

7. Resolved that the rights of suffrage [the method of election] in the first branch of the National Legislature ought . . . to be . . . according to some equitable ratio of representation, namely, in proportion to the whole number of white and other free citizens . . . & three fifths of all other persons [*i.e.*, slaves] . . . except Indians not paying taxes. . .

8. Resolved that the right of suffrage [the method of election] in the second branch of the National Legislature ought to be according to the rule established for the first.

9. Resolved that a National Executive be instituted to consist of a single person, to be chosen by the National Legislature for a term of seven years. . . .

10. Resolved that the National Executive shall have a right to negative [veto] any Legislative Act, which shall not be afterwards passed unless by two thirds of each branch of the National Legislature.

11. Resolved that a National Judiciary be established, to consist of one supreme tribunal [court], the Judges of which to be appointed by the second branch of the National Legislature, to hold their offices during good behaviour [*i.e.*, usually for life]. . . .

12. Resolved that the National Legislature be em-

powered to appoint inferior Tribunals [*i.e.*, lower federal courts]. . . .

17. Resolved that provision ought to be made for the amendment of the Articles of Union whensoever it shall seem necessary.

THE SMALL STATES REBEL

Elect a President for seven years. Let the people choose a House of Representatives, but have each state legislature choose its Senators. Have the entire plan accepted or rejected by state conventions elected by the people.

These were important tentative decisions reached early through the influence of Virginia, Pennsylvania, and the other large states. But then the nationalists went too far. On June 11 they won a close vote by which not only Representatives but also Senators would be chosen according to the number of inhabitants of a state—one man, one vote. The small states had wanted to be treated as equals of the large states; now they rebelled.

"The small states . . . would sooner submit to a foreign power," declared John Dickinson of Delaware, indignantly, "than . . . be deprived of an equality of suffrage [votes] in both branches of the legislature, and thereby be thrown under the domination of the large states."

Luther Martin of Maryland blustered, John Lansing spoke for the states' rights delegates of New York, Roger Sherman of Connecticut joined the protest.

On June 15 the small states struck back. William Paterson, a sawed-off little Irishman from New Jersey, presented a plan born of the fears of the small states that the nationalists were about to redraw the map—without any state lines! Paterson charged that the Virginia Plan would throw the states "into hotchpot."

His own plan turned the clock back. Instead of a new constitution it offered a face-lift for the old Articles of Confederation.

Let the "United States in Congress" now have the right to collect import duties and even to require that the states honor Congress' requests for money. Let Congress elect a committee to serve as an executive. But the individual states would remain sovereign and independent.

If the large states would not compromise, this New Jersey Plan might deadlock the Convention and force it to adjourn. Newspapers so optimistic about harmony in the Convention that they were about to call it "Unanimity Hall" would have a sad awakening for their readers.

The following selection is from the New Jersey Plan as printed in James Madison's *Debates in the Federal Convention of 1787* (first published 1900).

June 15

1. Resolved that the articles of Confederation ought to be so revised . . . as to render the federal Constitution adequate to the exigencies of Government, & the preservation of the Union.

2. Resolved that . . . the United States in Congress . . . be authorized to pass acts for raising a revenue, by levying a duty . . . on all goods . . . imported into any part of the United States, by Stamps on paper, vellum or parchment, and by a postage on all letters or packages. . . .

4. Resolved that the United States in Congress be authorized to elect a federal Executive to consist of [an unspecified number of] persons, to continue in office for the term of [an unspecified number of] years . . . to be . . . removable by Congress on application by a majority of the Executives of the several States. . . .

5. Resolved that a federal Judiciary be established to consist of a supreme Tribunal the Judges of which to be appointed by the Executive, & to hold their offices during good behaviour. . . .

6. Resolved that all Acts of the United States in Congress . . . and all Treaties made & ratified under the authority of the United States shall be the supreme law of the respective States so far forth as those Acts or Treaties shall relate to the said States or their Citizens. . . .

9. Resolved that a Citizen of one State committing an offence in another State of the Union, shall be deemed guilty of the same offence as if it had been committed by a Citizen of the State in which the offence was committed.

PRO AND CON

"How can we give the people something they haven't asked for? How can we expect them to accept it?"

This was the chief argument of those who opposed the Virginia Plan. The Convention had been called to *amend* the Articles of Confederation, not to scrap them. Delegates from Connecticut, New Jersey, and Delaware declared that the small states would "never confederate" under the new scheme.

But James Wilson, the learned Caledonian (Scotsman) from Pennsylvania, pushed his spectacles to the end of his nose and replied stoutly. The Convention, he said, was free to *"conclude* [decide] *nothing"* but it might *"propose anything."* Let the people decide afterward.

And James Madison showed that the New Jersey Plan

would not prevent the anarchy that threatened under the Articles of Confederation. Only a new constitution, establishing a direct relationship between the federal government and the citizens, could do that.

(By now it was clear that the Convention would last some time, so George Washington had written home requesting that his new umbrella be sent. "Have you thinned the Carrots which were too thick?" he asked his farm manager.)

The following selection gives important passages from the speeches of John Lansing, James Wilson, and James Madison; it is from James Madison's *Debates in the Federal Convention of 1787* (first published 1900).

June 16

Mr. LANSING called for the reading of the first resolution of each plan, which he considered as involving principles directly in contrast; that of Mr. Paterson [the New Jersey Plan] says he sustains the sovereignty of the respective States, that of Mr. Randolph [the Virginia Plan] destroys it: the latter requires a negative [power to veto] on all the laws of the particular States; the former, only certain general powers for the general good. The plan of Mr. Randolph in short absorbs all power except what may be exercised in the little local matters of the States. . . .

He [Mr. Lansing] grounded his preference for Mr. Paterson's plan, chiefly on two objections against that of Mr. Randolph. 1. want of power in the Convention to discuss & propose it. 2. the improbability of its being adopted.

1. He was decidedly of opinion that the power of the Convention was restrained to amendments of a federal nature, and having for their basis the Confederacy in being. . . . And this limitation of the power to an amendment of the Confederacy, marked

the opinion of the States, that it was unnecessary & improper to go farther. . . .

2. was it probable that the States would adopt & ratify a scheme, which they had never authorized us to propose? and which so far exceeded what they regarded as sufficient? [They had refused to accept] the plan of revenue proposed by Congress in 1783. . . . Can so great a change [in attitude] be supposed to have already taken place? . . .

Mr. WILSON . . . With regard to the *power of the Convention* [to make changes], he conceived himself authorized to *conclude nothing*, but to be at liberty to *propose any thing*. In this particular he felt himself perfectly indifferent to the two plans.

With *regard to the sentiments of the people*, he conceived it difficult to know precisely what they are. Those of the particular circle in which one moved, were commonly mistaken for the general voice. He could not persuade himself that the State Governments & Sovereignties were so much the idols of the people, nor a National Government so obnoxious to them, as some supposed.

Why should a National Government be unpopular? Has it less dignity? will each Citizen enjoy under it less liberty or protection? Will a Citizen of *Delaware* be degraded by becoming a Citizen of the *United States*? Where do the people look at present for relief from the evils of which they complain? Is it from an internal reform of their Governments? no, Sir. It is from the National Councils that relief is expected.

For these reasons he did not fear, that the people would not follow us into a national Government and it will be a further recommendation of Mr. Randolph's plan that it is to be submitted to *them*, and not to the *Legislatures*, for ratification.

Three days later James Madison tried to persuade the small states to accept the Virginia Plan.

Mr. MADISON . . . begged the smaller States which were most attached to Mr. Paterson's plan to consider . . . the situation in which they would remain in case their pertinacious adherence to an inadmissible plan should prevent the adoption of any plan. . . . Let the Union of the States be dissolved, and one of two consequences must happen. Either the States must remain individually independent & sovereign; or two or more Confederacies must be formed among them.

In the first event would the small States be more secure against the ambition & power of their larger neighbours, than they would be under a general Government . . . ? In the second, can the smaller expect that their larger neighbours would confederate with them on the principle of the present confederacy, which gives to each member, an equal suffrage [vote]; or that they would exact less severe concessions from the smaller States, than are proposed in the scheme of Mr. Randolph?

[Roll Call of the States]
On the question . . . whether the Committee should rise & Mr. Randolph's propositions be re-reported without alteration, which was in fact a question whether Mr. Randolph's should be adhered to as preferable to those of Mr. Paterson:

Massachusetts ay. Connecticut ay. New York no. New Jersey no. Pennsylvania ay. Delaware no. Maryland divided. Virginia ay. North Carolina ay. South Carolina ay. Georgia ay. [The Virginia Plan wins, 7–3.]

This vote simply meant that the Virginia Plan would continue to be discussed by the Convention, acting as a committee of the whole. It would not be replaced by the New Jersey Plan as the scheme to be debated. But, of course, any plan under discussion could be modified—and the small states were still determined to modify certain provisions of the Virginia Plan, especially the one about the election of Senators.

SHOULD AMERICA HAVE A KING?

Alexander Hamilton was a gifted nationalist delegate who did not contribute to the Convention as much as was expected. He was absent most of the time; perhaps he felt handcuffed by the two antinationalist New Yorkers, who could always outvote him. His one major speech, given during the debate over the New Jersey Plan, was astoundingly irrelevant.

"Why not establish a monarchy?" he asked, in effect. He proposed a senate that would represent only the rich and be chosen for life. And he proposed an *"elective Monarch"*—a President who would also hold office for life. In his notes, he even favored a hereditary monarch. Yet the one point that everyone agreed on was that America should be a republic.

Alexander Hamilton spoke for nearly six hours—a short, slender man with animated, mobile features, lifting his head defiantly. He was pleading for the most "high-toned" government of all! His speech, however, dropped into a deep well of silence. No one answered its arguments; no one even referred to it afterward.

Madison and Wilson, the nationalist leaders, may have been embarrassed by Hamilton's extremism. On the other hand, perhaps they thought that it would make the strong government of the Virginia Plan seem more like a compromise between Hamilton's monarchy and the remodeled Confederation of the New Jersey Plan.

The following selection is from Alexander Hamilton's speech of June 18, as recorded in James Madison's *Debates in the Federal Convention of 1787* (first published 1900).

June 18

Mr. HAMILTON . . . We ought to go as far in order to attain stability and permanency, as republican principles will admit. Let one branch of the Legislature hold their places for life or at least during good behaviour. Let the Executive also be for life. . . . On this plan we should have in the Senate a permanent will, a weighty interest, which would answer essential purposes.

But is this a Republican Government, it will be asked? Yes if all the Magistrates are appointed, and vacancies are filled, by the people, or a process of election originating with the people. . . .

It will be objected probably, that such an Executive [for life] will be an *elective Monarch*, and will give birth to the tumults which characterize that form of Government. He would reply that *Monarch* is an indefinite term. It marks not either the degree or duration of power. If this Executive Magistrate would be a monarch for life—the other proposed by the Report from the Committee of the whole, would be a monarch for seven years. . . .

It had been observed by judicious writers that elective monarchies would be the best if they could be guarded against the *tumults* excited by the ambition and intrigues of competitors. He was not sure that tumults were an inseparable evil. He rather thought this character [characteristic] of Elective

Monarchies had been taken rather from particular cases than from general principles.

The election of Roman Emperors was made by the *Army*. In *Poland* the election is made by great rival *princes* with independent power, and ample means, of raising commotions. In the German Empire, the appointment is made by the Electors & Princes, who have equal motives & means, for exciting cabals & parties. Might not such a mode of election be devised among ourselves as will defend the community against these effects?

Just eleven days later, June 29, Hamilton left Philadelphia. He made a flying visit to the Convention on August 13 but did not return to stay until September 6, in time for the closing ceremonies. The thirty-year-old Hamilton may have preferred the company of his beautiful dark-eyed wife Betsy, in New York, to that of the politicians in Philadelphia.

ONE STATE, ONE VOTE

At the end of June, the Convention had to decide on its most explosive issue. How many Representatives and how many Senators would each state have? This, as the shrewd Hamilton observed, was "a contest for power, not for liberty."

The large-state nationalists wanted the number to depend on the number of inhabitants, and they won their point for the House of Representatives. But the small states were insistent that in the Senate, at least, all states should be equal—one state, one vote.

"If the Large States . . . dissolve the Confederation," warned a fat, angry Gunning Bedford of Delaware, "the small ones will find some foreign ally . . . who will take them by the hand and do them justice!"

Luther Martin made a furious states' rights speech. James Madison replied, coolly asking what the small states were afraid of. Would their citizens be any less free if a one man, one vote principle were followed? Dr. William Johnson, a gracious, learned Connecticut delegate, pleaded for moderation.

The following selection gives key passages from the tense speeches of Luther Martin, James Madison, and Dr. William Johnson; it is from James Madison's *Debates in the Federal Convention of 1787* (first published 1900).

June 27

Mr. LUTHER MARTIN contended at great length and with great eagerness that the General Government was meant merely to preserve the State Governments: not to govern individuals: that its powers ought to be kept within narrow limits; that if too little power was given to it, more might be added; but that if too much, it could never be resumed: that individuals as such have little to do but with their own States . . . :

that to resort to the Citizens at large for their sanction to a new Government will be throwing them back into a State of Nature: that the dissolution of the State Governments is involved in the nature of the process: that the people have no right to do this without the consent of those to whom they have delegated their power for State purposes . . .—

that an equal vote in each State was essential to the federal idea, and was founded in justice & freedom, not merely in policy: that tho' the States may give up this right of sovereignty, yet they had not, and ought not . . .—

This was the substance of a speech which was con-

tinued more than three hours. He was too much ex-
hausted he said to finish his remarks, and reminded
the House that he should tomorrow, resume them.

The next morning, Luther Martin kept his promise.

Mr. LUTHER MARTIN resumed his discourse,
contending that the General Government ought to be
formed for the States, not for individuals: that if the
States were to have votes in proportion to their numbers of people, it would be the same thing whether
their representatives were chosen by the Legislatures
or the people; the smaller States would be equally
enslaved....

This was the substance of the residue of his discourse which was delivered with much diffuseness &
considerable vehemence....

Mr. MADISON . . . It is not necessary to secure
the small States against the large ones. . . . Was a
combination of the large ones. . . . dreaded? this must
arise either from some interest common to Virginia,
Massachusetts and Pennsylvania . . . or from the
mere circumstance of . . . size.

Did any such common interest exist? . . . In point
of manners, Religion, and the other [such] circumstances . . . they were not more assimilated [alike]
than the other States.—In point of the staple pro-
ductions they were as dissimilar as any three other
States in the Union. The Staple of Massachusetts was
fish, of Pennsylvania *flour*, of Virginia *Tobacco*.

Was a combination to be apprehended from the
mere circumstance . . . of size? . . . Experience rather
taught a contrary lesson. Among individuals of superior eminence & weight in Society, rivalships were
much more frequent than coalitions. Among inde-

pendent nations, pre-eminent over their neighbours, the same remark was verified. Carthage & Rome tore one another to pieces instead of uniting their forces to devour the weaker nations of the Earth. The Houses of Austria & France were hostile as long as they remained the greatest powers of Europe.

Madison continued this train of thought two days later, in another speech.

June 30

The States were divided into different interests not by their difference of size, but by other circumstances; the most material of which resulted partly from climate, but principally from the effects of their having or not having slaves . . . The great division of interests in the United States . . . did not lie between the large & small States: It lay between the Northern & Southern, and if any defensive power were necessary, it ought to be mutually given to these two interests.

Dr. William Johnson, son of the first president of King's College (Columbia) and just appointed president of Columbia himself, tried to mediate. He recommended the compromise favored by other Connecticut delegates: proportional representation in the House, but equal representation for each state in the Senate. But the large states were adamantly opposed to any compromise.

June 29

Doctor JOHNSON. The controversy must be endless whilst Gentlemen differ in the grounds of their arguments; Those on one side considering the States as districts of people composing one political Society; those on the other considering them as so many political societies.

The fact is that the States do exist as political Societies, and a Government is to be formed for them in their political capacity, as well as for the individuals composing them. Does it not seem to follow, that if the States as such are to exist they must be armed with some power of self-defense? . . .

On the whole he thought that as in some respects the States are to be considered in their political capacity, and in others as districts of individual citizens, the two ideas embraced on different sides, instead of being opposed to each other, ought to be combined; that in *one* branch the *people*, ought to be represented; in the *other* the *States*.

AN APPEAL TO GOD

Seeing that the large states and the small states were on a collision course, Benjamin Franklin moved that each day's session be opened with a prayer. Let the delegates lay aside their fears and conflicts for a few moments while they asked for "the assistance of Heaven"; then they might find a way afterward.

The following selection is from Benjamin Franklin's motion, as recorded in James Madison's *Debates in the Federal Convention of 1787* (first published 1900).

June 28

Mr. President

The small progress we have made after four or five weeks close attendance & continual reasonings with each other . . . is methinks a melancholy proof of the imperfection of the Human Understanding. We indeed seem to feel our own want of political wisdom, since we have been running about in search of it. We have gone back to ancient history for models of Government. . . . And we have viewed Modern States all round Europe, but find none of their Constitutions suitable to our circumstances.

In this situation . . . how has it happened, Sir, that we have not hitherto once thought of humbly applying to the Father of lights to illuminate our understandings? In the beginning of the Contest with Great Britain, when we were sensible of danger we had daily prayer in this room for the divine protection.—Our prayers, Sir, were heard, & they were graciously answered. . . . And have we now forgotten that powerful friend? or do we imagine that we no longer need his assistance?

I have lived, Sir, a long time, and the longer I live, the more convincing proofs I see of this truth—*that God Governs in the affairs of men.* And if a sparrow cannot fall to the ground without his notice, is it probable that an empire can rise without his aid? . . . [If we fail], mankind may hereafter from this unfortunate instance, despair of establishing Governments by Human wisdom and leave it to chance, war and conquest.

I therefore beg leave to move—that henceforth prayers imploring the assistance of Heaven, and its blessings on our deliberations, be held in this Assembly every morning before we proceed to business, and that one or more of the Clergy of this City be requested to officiate in that Service.

Roger Sherman from Puritan Connecticut quickly seconded the motion. But Alexander Hamilton worried that the public would view this action as a sign of "embarrassments and dissensions within the Convention." Hugh Williamson of North Carolina said they had no money with which to pay a minister. The deeper wartime emotions which had found relief in prayer in 1776 were not felt by this rationalist assembly. They adjourned without voting on Franklin's motion.

"Thought prayers unnecessary," Franklin noted dryly, in his journal.

CRISIS

The delegates were now in the eye of the storm. On July 2, a motion that each state have one vote in the Senate received a tie vote, 5–5. Thus the motion failed, but the large and small states remained deadlocked.

Within eight days the disaffected states' rights delegates from New York would walk out, leaving only eleven states represented. Within two weeks William Paterson of New Jersey would propose that the whole Convention go home—without having written a constitution. At the moment an unhappy James Madison and James Wilson were declaring that populous Virginia and Pennsylvania would not confederate if given no more Senators than tiny Delaware.

Luther Martin considered the Convention "on the verge of dissolution." And a visiting French officer who saw Washington leaving the stifling State House wrote: "The look on his face reminded me of its expression . . . in Valley Forge Camp."

"We are now at a full stop," said Roger Sherman of Connecticut. The bent ex-shoemaker then made an eleventh-hour suggestion for saving the Convention—and the American Republic.

The following selection gives the tie-vote roll call, Sherman's motion, and the response to it; it is from James Madison's *Debates in the Federal Convention of 1787* (first published 1900).

[Roll Call of the States]

On the question for allowing each State one vote in the second branch. . . . Massachusetts no. Connecticut ay. New York ay. New Jersey ay. Pennsylvania no. Delaware ay. Maryland ay. . . . Virginia no. North Carolina no. South Carolina no. Georgia divided. . . . [A 5–5 tie—the motion fails.]

Mr. SHERMAN. We are now at a full stop, and nobody he supposed meant that we should break up without doing something. A committee he thought most likely to hit on some expedient. . . .

Mr. GERRY was for the Commitment [to a committee]. Something must be done, or we shall disappoint not only America, but the whole world. He suggested a consideration of the State we should be thrown into by the failure of the Union. We should be without an Umpire to decide controversies and must be at the mercy of events. What too is to become of our treaties—what of our foreign debts, what of our domestic? We must make concessions on both sides. Without these the Constitutions of the several States would never have been formed. . . .

The Committee elected by ballot, were Mr. Gerry, Mr. Ellsworth, Mr. Yates, Mr. Paterson, Dr. Franklin, Mr. Bedford, Mr. Martin, Mr. Mason, Mr. Davie, Mr. Rutledge, Mr. Baldwin.

This committee consisted of one member from each of the eleven states represented in the Convention. Rhode Island had sent no one, and the delegates from New Hampshire had not yet arrived. Roger Sherman replaced Oliver Ellsworth for Connecticut when Ellsworth became ill.

THE ART OF COMPROMISE

*If we do not agree on this middle &
moderate ground he [Oliver Ellsworth] was
afraid we . . . should fly into a variety of
shapes & directions, and most probably into
several confederations and not without bloodshed.*

—OLIVER ELLSWORTH

A BARGAIN IS STRUCK

"When you are in a minority, talk," said canny Roger Sherman; "when you are in a majority, vote." This Connecticut Yankee delegate *had* talked, in defense of the small states. Many historians give him credit for being the first to suggest the compromise the committee now recommended to the Convention: that each state be given representatives in proportion to its population in the House, but that each state have an equal vote in the Senate.

To pacify the large states, the committee also recommended that all money bills originate in the House, which the large states would dominate. (Americans were touchy about taxes.)

Madison, Wilson, and their followers were not pacified. They thought the committee was suggesting that mountains and meadows be represented, not men. Only the more sensitive among the large-state delegates perceived that their colleagues from the small states really were frightened. Men from Delaware, or Maryland, or New Jersey believed, with Dr. Johnson of Connecticut, that the states "do [already] exist as political Societies." The states could not be ignored or abolished. Indeed, it had been a committee member from populous Pennsylvania, Benjamin Franklin, who made the motion for the "Great Compromise."

For a week, there was a final, no-holds-barred debate. All the New Yorkers had departed. Madison and Wilson braced themselves against compromise. Luther Martin threatened that there might be *two* confederacies instead

102

of one—the small states would form their own. Sherman, Gerry, and Caleb Strong of Massachusetts pleaded for coolness and reason.

At last, on July 16, by the narrowest of margins, the Convention voted to adopt the committee's recommendations. The small states had won.

The following selection includes high points of the debate and the vote. If the Great Compromise had lost, there would have been no Constitution. The selection is from James Madison's *Debates in the Federal Convention of 1787* (first published 1900).

July 5

Mr. GERRY delivered in from the Committee appointed on Monday last the following Report.

"The Committee . . . submit the following Report: That the subsequent propositions be recommended to the Convention on condition that both shall be generally adopted.

"I. that in the first branch of the Legislature each of the States now in the Union shall be allowed one member for every 40,000 inhabitants . . . : that each State not containing that number shall be allowed one member: that all bills for raising or appropriating money, and for fixing the Salaries of the officers of the Government of the United States shall originate in the first branch of the Legislature, and shall not be altered or amended by the second branch. . . .

"II. That in the second branch each State shall have an equal vote."

Mr. GERRY. Tho' he had assented to the Report in the Committee, he had very material objections to it. We were however in a peculiar situation. We were neither the same Nation nor different Nations. We ought not therefore to pursue the one or the other of these ideas too closely. If no compromise should take place what will be the consequence? A secession he foresaw would take place. . . . If we do not come to some agreement among ourselves some foreign sword will probably do the work for us. . . .

Mr. MASON. The consideration which weighed with the Committee was that the first branch [House of Representatives] would be the immediate representatives of the people, the second would not. Should the latter have the power of giving away the people's money, they might soon forget the source from whence they received it. We might soon have an aristocracy. . . . He was a friend to proportional representation in both branches; but supposed that some points must be yielded for the sake of accommodation.

July 6

Doctor FRANKLIN did not mean to go into a justification of the Report; but as it had been asked what would be the use of restraining the second branch [Senate] from meddling with money bills, he could not but remark that it was always of importance that the people should know who had disposed of their money, & how it had been disposed of. . . . This end would, he thought, be best attained, if money affairs were to be confined to the immediate representatives of the people.

July 7

Mr. PATERSON . . . The small States would never be able to defend themselves without an equality of votes in the second branch [Senate]. There was no other ground of accommodation. His resolution was fixed. He would meet the large States on that Ground and no other. . . .

Mr. GOUVERNEUR MORRIS . . . On the declaration of Independence, a Government was to be formed. The small States aware of the necessity of preventing anarchy, and taking advantage of the moment, extorted from the large ones an equality of votes. Standing now on that ground, they demand under the new system greater rights as men, than their fellow Citizens of the large States. The proper answer to them is that the same necessity . . . does not now exist, and that the large States are at liberty now to consider what is right, rather than what may be expedient. . . .

What if all the Charters & Constitutions of the States were thrown into the fire, and all their demagogues into the ocean? What would it be to the happiness of America? [It would not matter in the least.]

July 14

Mr. WILSON traced the progress of the report . . . remarking that . . . on the question concerning an equality of votes . . . our Constituents had they voted as their representatives did, would have stood as two-thirds against the equality, and one-third only in favor of it [*i.e.*, the delegates of the larger states represented more constituents than the delegates of the smaller states]. . . . What hopes will our Constituents entertain when they find that the essential principles of justice have been violated in the outset of the Government? . . .

Mr. L. MARTIN denies that there were two-thirds against the equality of votes. The States that please to call themselves large, are the weakest in the Union. Look at Massachusetts. Look at Virginia. Are they efficient States? He was for letting a separation take place if they desired it. He had rather there should be two Confederacies, than one founded on any other principle than an equality of votes in the second branch [Senate] at least.

Mr. WILSON was not surprised that those who say that a minority is more than the majority should say that the minority is stronger than the majority. He supposed the next assertion will be that they are richer also; though he hardly expected it would be persisted in when the States shall be called on for taxes & troops. . . .

Mr. STRONG. The Convention had been much divided in opinion. In order to avoid the consequences of it, an accommodation had been proposed. . . . It is agreed on all hands that Congress are nearly at an end. If no Accommodation takes place, the Union itself must soon be dissolved. It has been suggested that if we can not come to any general agreement, the principal States may form & recommend a scheme of Government. But will the small States in that case ever accede to it? . . .

He thought the small States had made a considerable concession in the article of money bills; and that they might naturally expect some concessions on the other side. From this view of the matter he was compelled to give his vote for the Report taken all together.

[Roll Call of the States]

July 16

On the question for agreeing to the whole Report as amended & including the equality of votes in the second branch. It passed in the Affirmative.

Massachusetts divided. . . . Connecticut ay. New Jersey ay. Pennsylvania no. Delaware ay. Maryland ay. Virginia no. North Carolina ay. . . . South Carolina no. Georgia no. [Equality of states in the Senate wins, 5–4.]

WALKOUT?

After the vote on the Great Compromise was taken, July 16, many of the large-state delegates were very upset. That same day Edmund Randolph of Virginia expressed their chagrin at an outcome which "had embarrassed the business extremely." Stiffly, he suggested that the Convention adjourn to give the small states a chance to think over what they had done—and repent!

William Paterson of New Jersey promptly retorted that the small states had no thought of "conciliation" if by that word Mr. Randolph meant they should give up their equal vote in the Senate. He offered to second a motion to end the Convention.

Angry and apprehensive as many delegates were, they were stunned by this proposal. Suddenly, they saw themselves standing on the brink of a precipice. The following selection reveals the turbulent emotions of this moment; it is from James Madison's *Debates in the Federal Convention of 1787* (first published 1900).

July 16

Mr. RANDOLPH. The vote of this morning [giving the states equal votes in the Senate] had embarrassed the business extremely. All the powers given in the Report from the Committee of the whole, were founded on the supposition that a Proportional representation was to prevail in both branches of the Legislature. . . . He wished the Convention might adjourn, that the large States might consider the steps proper to be taken in the present solemn crisis . . . and that the small States might also deliberate on the means of conciliation.

Mr. PATERSON, thought with Mr. Randolph that it was high time for the Convention to adjourn. . . . No conciliation could be admissible on the part of the smaller States on any other ground than that of an equality of votes in the second branch. If Mr. Randolph would reduce to form his motion for an adjournment sine die [a permanent adjournment], he would second it with all his heart.

General PINCKNEY wished to know of Mr. Randolph whether he meant an adjournment sine die, or only an adjournment for the day. If the former was meant, it differed much from his idea. He could not think of going to South Carolina and returning again to this place. . . .

Mr. RANDOLPH, had never entertained an idea of an adjournment sine die; & was sorry that his meaning had been so readily & strangely misinterpreted. He had in view merely an adjournment till tomorrow. . . .

Mr. PATERSON seconded the adjournment till tomorrow. . . .

On the morning following [July 17] before the hour of the convention a number of the members from the larger States . . . met for the purpose of consulting on the proper steps to be taken. . . . Several members from the [smaller] States also attended. The time was wasted in vague conversation on the subject, without any specific proposition or agreement. . . . It is probable that the result of this consultation satisfied the smaller States that they had nothing to apprehend from a union of the larger, in any plan whatever against the equality of votes in the second branch [Senate].

INTERMISSION

After the delegates agreed to remain in Philadelphia, things went better. The large states finally reconciled themselves to equality in the Senate, and the small states, in return, became very cooperative in other matters. By the end of July the delegates had debated all the resolutions of the Virginia Plan and were ready to turn the results over to a Committee of Detail, which would draw up a rough draft of the Constitution. The Convention adjourned July 26, for eleven days, while the Committee of Detail did its work.

Some delegates, like Roger Sherman and Dr. Johnson of Connecticut, dashed home for a short visit. General Charles Coatesworth Pinckney of South Carolina, who had brought two fine bay geldings with him, trotted out to nearby Bethlehem sightseeing.

One daring group at some time during the summer— perhaps in this interlude—boarded John Fitch's smoke-belching *Perseverance*. Manfully repressing their qualms, they went for a cruise on this pioneer steamship.

George Washington went fishing. On Monday and Tuesday, July 30 and 31, he traveled up near Valley Forge with Gouverneur Morris and cast for trout. He noted sadly that his old camp was all overgrown and that the forge itself was in ruins. Rain drove the party back to Philadelphia, but that weekend Washington journeyed to Trenton. Here he not only admired the Trenton Iron Works but made a good catch of perch.

While Washington was off fishing, other delegates attended a performance at the Opera House in Philadelphia. They sat through a concert, a "Comic Lecture" in five acts, and a "Comic Opera" in two acts. Perhaps these delegates were just as glad to return to their labors in the State House on August 6!

THE STAIN OF SLAVERY

From time to time, both before and after the adjournment, a shadow fell over the deliberations of the delegates. When they discussed how many representatives each state should have in the House—how the population of a state was to be computed—they came face to face with black slaves laboring in the fields of free America.

What should be done about slavery in the Constitution of a republic? Northerners squirmed uncomfortably at the thought of the "nefarious institution"; it had been abolished in Rhode Island and Massachusetts and was being phased out in the other New England states and Pennsylvania. Southerners became defensive. The South Carolinians wanted the blacks to count the same as free inhabitants so the Southern states would have more representatives in the House. South Carolina and especially Georgia wished to continue to import slaves to work their sparsely settled lands.

The issues were raised in July, uneasily compromised, then raised again in August. Another crisis threatened. But perhaps because the delegates were tiring, a compromise was accepted. In the census a slave would count as three-fifths of a freeman. Slaves imported from abroad could be taxed like other "goods"—but after 1800 (changed to 1808) the slave trade could be (and was) prohibited.

Could the delegates have done more? It is a moot question. Like Lincoln three-quarters of a century later, they placed the Union ahead of social reforms. To hold the Southern states, the North had to give some ground. (But James Madison and George Mason of Virginia violently denounced slavery.) Also, even the strongest antislavery men, while they despised the institution, seem scarcely to have thought of the slaves themselves as persons and pos-

110

sible equals. However, they were so disturbed by the situation that they avoided using the words "slave" or "slavery" in the Constitution. Slaves were "Person[s] held to Service or Labour" or "all other Persons" (in addition to freemen) or "such persons as the several states shall think proper to admit."

The fiery debates on slavery were an ominous harbinger of the blood to be shed at Gettysburg. The following selection gives high points; it is from James Madison's *Debates in the Federal Convention of 1787* (first published 1900).

July 11

Mr. BUTLER & General PINCKNEY insisted that blacks be included in the rule of Representation, *equally* with the Whites: and for that purpose moved that the words "three fifths" be struck out.

Mr. GERRY thought that three fifths of them was to say the least the full proportion that could be admitted.

Mr. GORHAM. This ratio was fixed by Congress as a rule of taxation. Then it was urged by the Delegates representing the States having slaves that the blacks were still more inferior to freemen. At present when the ratio of representation is to be established, we are assured that they are equal to freemen. The arguments on the former occasion had convinced him that three-fifths was pretty near the just proportion and he should vote according to the same opinion now. . . .

Mr. WILSON did not well see on what principle the admission of blacks in the proportion of three fifths could be explained. Are they admitted as Citizens? then why are they not admitted on an equality with White Citizens? are they admitted as property? then why is not other property admitted into the

111

computation? These were difficulties however which he thought must be overruled by the necessity of compromise. . . .

Mr. GOUVERNEUR MORRIS was compelled to declare himself reduced to the dilemma of doing injustice to the Southern States or to human nature, and he must therefore do it to the former. For he could never agree to give such encouragement to the slave trade as would be given by allowing them a representation for their negroes.

July 12

Mr. PINCKNEY moved to amend Mr. Randolph's motion so as to make "blacks equal to the whites in the ratio of representation." This he urged was nothing more than justice. The blacks are the labourers, the peasants of the Southern States: they are as productive of pecuniary resources as those of the Northern States.

The speeches above were given in July, when the preliminary decision about how slaves were to be counted was made. In August the subject came up again in the Committee of Detail's rough draft of the complete Constitution. The delegates went through this rough draft article by article. When they reached the articles dealing with how slaves should be counted, the following controversy erupted.

August 8

Mr. GOUVERNEUR MORRIS moved to insert "free" before the word inhabitants. . . . He never would concur in upholding domestic slavery. It was a nefarious institution. It was the curse of heaven on the States where it prevailed. Compare the free regions of the Middle States, where a rich & noble cultivation marks the prosperity & happiness of the people, with the misery & poverty which overspread the barren wastes of Virginia, Maryland, & the other States having slaves. . . . Proceed southwardly & every step you take thro' the great region of slaves presents a desert increasing, with the increasing proportion of these wretched beings.

Upon what principle is it that the slaves shall be computed in the representation? Are they men? Then make them Citizens and let them vote. Are they property? Why then is no other property included? The Houses in this city [Philadelphia] are worth more than all the wretched slaves which cover the rice swamps of South Carolina.

The admission of slaves into the Representation when fairly explained comes to this: that the inhabitant of Georgia and South Carolina who goes to the Coast of Africa, and in defiance of the most sacred laws of humanity tears away his fellow creatures from their dearest connections & damns them to the most cruel bondages, shall have more votes in a Government instituted for protection of the rights of mankind, than the Citizen of Pennsylvania or New Jersey who views with a laudable horror, so nefarious a practice. . . .

He would sooner submit himself to a tax for paying for all the negroes in the United States, than saddle posterity with such a Constitution.

Morris' motion lost. Later in August the question of allowing or prohibiting the importation of more slaves was discussed.

August 21

Mr. RUTLEDGE . . . Religion & humanity had nothing to do with this question [of the slave trade].

Interest alone is the governing principle with nations. The true question at present is whether the Southern States shall or shall not be parties to the Union. If the Northern States consult their interest, they will not oppose the increase of Slaves which will increase the commodities of which they will become the carriers. . . .

Mr. PINCKNEY. South Carolina can never receive the plan if it prohibits the slave trade. In every proposed extension of the powers of the Congress, that State has expressly & watchfully excepted that of meddling with the importation of negroes. If the States be all left at liberty on this subject, South Carolina may perhaps by degrees do of herself what is wished. . . .

August 22

Colonel MASON. This infernal traffic originated in the avarice of British Merchants. The British Government constantly checked the attempts of Virginia to put a stop to it. The present question concerns not the importing States alone but the whole Union. . . .

Maryland & Virginia he said had already prohibited the importation of slaves expressly. North Carolina had done the same in substance. All this would be in vain if South Carolina & Georgia be at liberty to import. The Western people are already calling out for slaves for their new lands, and will fill that Country with slaves if they can be got thro' South Carolina & Georgia.

Slavery discourages arts & manufactures. The poor despise labor when performed by slaves. They prevent the immigration of Whites, who really enrich & strengthen a Country. They produce the most pernicious effect on manners. Every master of slaves is born a petty tyrant. They bring the judgment of heaven on a Country. . . .

114

He held it essential in every point of view that the General Government should have power to prevent the increase of slavery.

George Mason's denunciation of slavery was made a week before the final compromise (August 29) which allowed importation of slaves to continue until 1800 (changed to 1808). Mason's speech had little or no effect.

HOW MUCH POWER
SHOULD A PRESIDENT HAVE?

In addition to slavery, another problem the delegates wrestled with early was that of the Chief Executive. They couldn't agree on how long he should be in office, whether he could be reelected, and especially how he should be chosen in the first place. But they quickly decided that he should be an independent and powerful figure. The enterprising classes represented in the Convention were tired of the muddling-through ways of the weak Confederation.

Besides, everyone knew that the first President would be George Washington, whom they trusted. Very well— let the President oversee the laws, make high appointments (to be confirmed by the Senate) and be commander in chief of the armed forces. Let him veto bills passed by Congress if he considered them bad, and make his opponents muster a two-thirds majority to override his veto. At least one delegate thought the President might order the armed forces into action in an emergency without consulting Congress.

Not all the powers and limitations of the Presidency were spelled out; an energetic President would have more influence than an inactive one. In general, the balance between an independent executive and Congress resembled that between an eighteenth-century English king and Parliament.

In the following selection, Gouverneur Morris develops the idea of a strong executive; the selection is from James Madison's *Debates in the Federal Convention of 1787* (first published 1900).

July 19

Mr. GOUVERNEUR MORRIS. It is necessary to take into one view all that relates to the establishment of the Executive; on the due formation of which must depend the efficacy & utility of the Union among the present and future States. It has been a maxim in Political Science that Republican Government is not adapted to a large extent of Country, because the energy of the Executive Magistracy can not reach the extreme parts of it. Our Country is an extensive one. We must either then renounce the blessings of the Union, or provide an Executive with sufficient vigor to pervade every part of it. . . .

One great object of the Executive is to control the Legislature. The Legislature will continually seek to aggrandize & perpetuate themselves; and will seize those critical moments produced by war, invasion or convulsion for that purpose. It is necessary then that the Executive Magistrate should be the guardian of the people, even of the lower classes, against Legislative tyranny, against the Great & the wealthy who in the course of things will necessarily compose the Legislative body.

Wealth tends to corrupt the mind & to nourish its love of power, and to stimulate it to oppression. History proves this to be the spirit of the opulent. . . . The Executive therefore ought to be so constituted as to be the great protector of the Mass of the people.

Later the Convention rejected a requirement that candidates for President be rich men worth at least $100,000. The young South Carolina aristocrat Charles Pinckney made this proposal; Benjamin Franklin rebutted it—expressing the democratic sentiments of the majority.

August 10

Doctor FRANKLIN expressed his dislike of every thing that tended to debase the spirit of the common people. If honesty was often the companion of wealth, and if poverty was exposed to peculiar temptation, it was not less true that the possession of property increased the desire of more property. Some of the greatest rogues he was ever acquainted with, were the richest rogues. We should remember the character which the Scripture requires in Rulers, that they should be men hating covetousness. This Constitution will be much read and attended to in Europe, and if it should betray a great partiality to the rich, will not only hurt us in the esteem of the most liberal and enlightened men there, but discourage the common people from removing to this Country.

The rough draft of the Constitution, presented by the Committee of Detail, gave Congress the power to declare war. There was a brief discussion of this clause, and the question of whether the President by himself could declare war was brought up. This foreshadowed a twentieth-century conflict between the President and the Congress on this very matter.

August 17

The clause "to make war"

Mr. PINCKNEY opposed the vesting this power in the Legislature. Its proceedings were too slow. It

117

would meet but once a year. The House of Representatives would be too numerous for such deliberations. The Senate would be the best depository, being more acquainted with foreign affairs. . . .

Mr. BUTLER. The objections against the Legislature lie in great degree against the Senate. He was for vesting the power in the President, who will have all the requisite qualities, and will not make war but when the Nation will support it. . . .

Mr. SHERMAN thought it stood very well. The Executive should be able to repel and not to commence war. . . .

Mr. GERRY never expected to hear in a republic a motion to empower the Executive alone to declare war. . . .

Mr. MASON was against giving the power of war to the Executive, because not safely to be trusted with it; or to the Senate, because not so constructed as to be entitled to it. He was for clogging rather than facilitating war; but for facilitating peace.

HOW TO ELECT A PRESIDENT

The Convention created a strong President, but its members were as baffled as Congressmen and commentators today over how to elect him. By popular vote? By a complicated electoral college? By Congress itself?

At first the delegates were inclined to have Congress ("the National Legislature") do the job. But might that not lead to deals between candidates and the legislators? Wouldn't it violate the principle of the separation of powers and make the executive dependent on the legislature?

One aristocrat, Gouverneur Morris, and one democrat, James Wilson, put their heads together and astounded everyone by suggesting that the people choose the President. Then he would represent the people against special interests of the wealthy class, which might be influential in Congress. But the delegates would not go that far toward democracy. The American Revolution had opened the doors of government to the people, but their full participation still lay in the future.

Then what about a kind of Mr. America contest? asked John Dickinson. Let each state nominate its "best citizen," and then Congress could select one of the thirteen as President.

This proposal aroused little enthusiasm. In despair or in a moment of cynicism, James Wilson suggested that a handful of members of Congress be chosen—"by lot"! These electors could then choose a President.

At last, after casting sixty ballots on the subject without reaching an agreement, the Convention threw up its hands and called on a Committee of Eleven to settle "postponed matters." This committee recommended that each state legislature provide a certain number of electors —the same number as the state's Representatives and Senators combined. These electors would meet and choose a President, but if no candidate received a majority of votes, the Senate would choose from among the five highest.

A weary Convention accepted this solution—except that it gave the House the right to decide an inconclusive election, with each state delegation there having just one vote. This is the basis of our system today.

The following selection gives high points of the debates and the final plan; it is from James Madison's *Debates in the Federal Convention of 1787* (first published 1900).

July 17

Mr. GOUVERNEUR MORRIS was pointedly against his [the President's] being so chosen [by

Congress]. He will be the mere creature of the Legislature: if appointed & impeachable by that body. He ought to be elected by the people at large, by the freeholders of the Country. . . . If the people should elect, they will never fail to prefer some man of distinguished character, or services; some man . . . of continental reputation.—If the Legislature elect, it will be the work of intrigue, of cabal, and of faction; . . . real merit will rarely be the title to the appointment. . . .

Mr. SHERMAN thought that the sense of the Nation would be better expressed by the Legislature, than by the people at large. The latter will never be sufficiently informed of characters, and besides will never give a majority of votes to any one man. They will generally vote for some man in their own State, and the largest State will have the best chance for the appointment. . . .

Mr. WILSON. Two arguments have been urged against an election of the Executive Magistrate by the people. The first is the example of Poland where an Election of the supreme Magistrate is attended with the most dangerous commotions. The cases he observed were totally dissimilar. The Polish nobles have resources & dependents which enable them to . . . threaten the Republic as well as each other. In the next place the electors all assemble in one place: which would not be the case with us. The second argument is that a *majority* of the people would never concur. It might be answered that the concurrence of a majority of people is not a necessary principle of election, nor required as such in any of the States. . . . A particular objection with him against an absolute election by the Legislature was that the Executive in that case would be too dependent to stand the mediator between the intrigues & sinister views of the Representatives and the general liberties & interests of the people.

Mr. PINCKNEY did not expect this question would again have been brought forward; An Election by the people being liable to the most obvious & striking objections. They will be led by a few active & designing men. The most populous States by combining in favor of the same individual will be able to carry their points. The National Legislature being most immediately interested in the laws made by themselves, will be most attentive to the choice of a fit man to carry them properly into execution.

It was the end of August when the Convention appointed the Committee of Eleven to make up its mind for it. The committee reported back on September 4. The final plan, voted September 6, reads as follows.

September 6

He [the President] shall . . . be elected in the following manner.

Each State shall appoint in such manner as its Legislature may direct, a number of electors equal to the whole number of Senators and members of the House of Representatives, to which the State may be entitled in the Legislature. . . .

The Electors shall meet in their respective States and vote by ballot for two persons, of whom one at least shall not be an inhabitant of the same State with themselves [and they shall transmit the results to the President of the Senate]. . . .

The person having the greatest number of votes shall be the President (if such number be a majority of the whole number of electors appointed). . . . But if no person have a majority, then from the five high-

est on the list, the House of Representatives shall . . .
choose by ballot the President.

IS THIS VICE PRESIDENT NECESSARY?

At the very moment that they were inventing the office
of Vice President a few delegates wondered if it were
needed. Some thought the Vice President's presiding over
the Senate would give the President too much influence
in the legislature, also.

But if the Vice President didn't wield the gavel, what
else was there for him to do—except wait, one heartbeat
away, for a disaster to strike the President?

The following selection contains some comments about
an office that has been more discussed since 1787 than it
was at the time. The selection is from James Madison's
Debates in the Federal Convention of 1787 (first published 1900).

September 7

Mr. GERRY opposed this regulation. We might as
well put the President himself at the head of the
Legislature. The close intimacy that must subsist between the President & vice-president makes it absolutely improper. He was against having any vice
President.

Mr. GOUVERNEUR MORRIS. The vice president then will be the first heir apparent that ever
loved his father. If there should be no vice president,
the President of the Senate would be temporary suc-
cessor, which would amount to the same thing.

Mr. SHERMAN saw no danger in the case. If the
vice-President were not to be President of the Senate, he would be without employment, and some

member by being made President must be deprived of his vote, unless when an equal division of votes might happen in the Senate, which would be but seldom.

Mr. RANDOLPH concurred in the opposition to the clause.

Mr. WILLIAMSON, observed that such an officer as vice-President was not wanted [needed]. He was introduced only for the sake of a valuable mode of election which required two to be chosen at the same time.

Colonel MASON, thought the office of vice-President an encroachment on the rights of the Senate; and that it mixed too much the Legislative & Executive, which . . . ought to be kept as separate as possible.

A MINORITY PLEA

The Constitutional Convention did not discuss religion. Its members were writing "positive law," the rules for a limited federal government, not "natural law," dealing with man's inalienable rights. The state constitutions were thought to guarantee these inalienable rights, including freedom of religion.

But Americans outside the Convention were much concerned about these rights, especially Americans belonging to minorities. So when a rumor was heard that the Convention would require a religious test for federal officeholders, a patriotic Jew, Jonas Phillips, wrote an anxious letter "to the President and Members of the Convention."

Jonas Phillips, a Philadelphia merchant who had

fought in the Revolution, asked the Convention to change the religious requirement for officeholders in the Pennsylvania constitution. That constitution required that representatives accept the New Testament as "given by a divine inspiration"—something a Jew could not do. Some other state constitutions barred non-Protestants from office.

The Constitutional Convention, of course, had no power to change any state constitution. But what Jonas Phillips was really worried about was the possibility that a religious test might be included in the new national constitution. His letter was a strong indirect plea against such a test.

The following selection is from Jonas Phillips' letter (from Max Farrand, ed., *The Records of the Federal Convention of 1787*, III).

September 7

I the subscriber [undersigned] being one of the people called Jews of the City of Philadelphia, a people scattered and dispersed among all nations, do behold with Concern that among the laws in the Constitution of Pennsylvania there is a Clause Sect. 10 . . . viz. "I do believe in one God the Creator and governour of the universe, the Rewarder of the good and the punisher of the wicked—and I do acknowledge the scriptures of the old and New testament to be given by a divine inspiration."

To swear and believe that the new testament was given by divine inspiration is absolutely against the Religious principle of a Jew, and is against his Conscience to take any such oath. By the above law a Jew is deprived of holding any public office or place of Government which is a Contradictory to the bill of Right[s] Sect. 2. . . .

It is well known among all the Citizens of the thirteen united States that the Jews have been true and faithful whigs, and during the late Contest with England they have been foremost in aiding and assisting the States with their lives and fortunes, they have supported the Cause, have bravely fought and bled for liberty which they Can not Enjoy.

Therefore if the honourable Convention shall in their Wisdom think fit and alter the said oath and leave out the words . . . viz. "and I do acknowledge the scripture of the new testament to be given by divine inspiration"—then the Israelites will think them sel[ves] happy to live under a government where all Religious societies are on an Equal footing. I solicit this favour for my self, my Children and posterity and for the benefit of all the Israelites through the thirteen united States of america.

Whether intentionally or not, the Convention answered Jonas Phillips' plea in Article VI of the Constitution, which states that "no religious Test shall ever be required as a Qualification to any Office or public Trust under the United States."

The Convention also defended another minority, the scattered backwoodsmen. Aristocratic Gouverneur Morris wished to change the provisions of the Northwest Ordinance, which admitted new states on a basis of equality. Morris thought the backwoodsmen would "inevitably bring on a war with Spain for the Mississippi." He wished to check their power by basing new states' representation in Congress on property rather than population—this would favor the wealthy East.

But the Convention refused to go along with Morris and kept the equality provisions of the Northwest Ordinance. It left any future change up to Congress.

"We are providing for our posterity, for our children & our grand Children, who would be as likely to be citizens

125

of new Western States, as of the old States," said Roger Sherman.

POWER TO THE PEOPLE

The eighteenth century is called the Age of Reason. The American Constitution was the work of reasonable men, skilled in the art of compromise. Three crucial compromises brought it into being: between large and small states; between free and slave states; between champions of centralized and of local government.

But the eighteenth century was also the century when a romantic faith in the powers of the common man swept over the Western world. Republicanism had its roots, as we have seen, in the views of earlier thinkers, especially John Locke. And republicanism triumphed in the method the Convention adopted for having the Constitution ratified.

Locke had taught that in the beginning people got together to form a government by a "compact"; they agreed to allow chosen representatives to rule them in order to protect their persons and property. So the Convention voted not to *impose* the new government through Congress or state legislatures, but to *submit* it to a convention in each state chosen by the people. Let the people, not the politicians, decide.

"Conventions of the people or with power derived expressly from the people, were not . . . thought of" before, complained a conservative opponent of this "new set of ideas." By voting power to the people, the Convention cut any remaining links with the old Articles of Confederation.

The following selection gives the debate on this topic; it is from James Madison's *Debates in the Federal Convention of 1787* (first published 1900).

July 23

Colonel MASON considered a reference of the plan to the authority of the people as one of the most important and essential of the Resolutions. The [State] Legislatures have no power to ratify it. They are the mere creatures of the State Constitutions, and can not be greater than their creators. And he knew of no power in any of the Constitutions . . . that could be competent to this object.

Whither then must we resort? To the people with whom all power remains that has not been given up in the Constitutions derived from them. It was of great moment he observed that this doctrine should be cherished as the basis of free Government. . . .

Mr. RANDOLPH. One idea has pervaded all our proceedings, to wit, that opposition as well from the States as from individuals, will be made to the System to be proposed. . . . Whose opposition will be most likely to be excited against the System? That of the local demagogues who will be degraded by it from the importance they now hold. These will spare no efforts to impede that progress in the popular mind which will be necessary to the adoption of the plan. . . .

It is of great importance therefore that the consideration of this subject should be transferred from the Legislatures where this class of men, have their full influence to a field in which their efforts can be less mischievous. . . .

Mr. GERRY. The arguments of Colonel Mason & Mr. Randolph prove too much. . . . Great confusion he was confident would result from a recurrence to the people. They would never agree on any thing. . . .

Mr. GORHAM was against referring the plan to the Legislatures. 1. Men chosen by the people for the particular purpose, will discuss the subject more

127

candidly than members of the Legislature who are to lose the power which is to be given up to the General Government. 2. Some of the Legislatures are composed of several branches. It will consequently be more difficult in these cases to get the plan through the Legislatures, than thro' a Convention. 3. [In] the States many of the ablest men are excluded from the Legislatures, but may be elected into a Convention. Among these may be ranked many of the Clergy who are generally friends to good Government....

Mr. ELLSWORTH ... He thought more was to be expected from the Legislatures than from the people. ... He observed that a new set of ideas seemed to have crept in since the articles of Confederation were established. Conventions of the people, or with power derived expressly from the people, were not then thought of. The Legislatures were considered as competent. Their ratification has been acquiesced in without complaint. To whom have Congress applied on subsequent occasions for further power? To the Legislatures; not to the people.

RUMBLINGS OF DISCONTENT

After the delegates had revised the rough draft of the Constitution, they handed it over to a Committee of Style. Gouverneur Morris did most of the polishing of the Constitution for this committee. He used "the plain, common language of mankind."

One of his happiest changes was in the preamble. The rough draft read: "We the People of the States of New Hampshire, Massachusetts" etc.—naming them all—"do ordain, declare, and establish the following Constitution. . . ." Morris changed this to "We the People of the United States" and added "in order to form a more perfect Union, to establish Justice, insure domestic Tranquillity, provide for the common defense, promote the general Welfare, and secure the Blessings of Liberty to ourselves and our Posterity, do ordain and establish this Constitution. . . ."

So the Convention neared its goal. But as it did so, a few extreme republicans became more and more distressed. Several, including Robert Yates and John Lansing of New York, John Mercer and Luther Martin of Maryland, had departed. Those who remained—and now Edmund Randolph joined them—thought that the nationalists were betraying the ideals of the American Revolution. What did Bunker Hill, Valley Forge, and Yorktown stand for if not for the struggle of *local* patriots against a distant tyranny? Why establish another highly centralized government which might also develop into a tyranny?

Why had there been no discussion of a bill of rights, to protect the people? Why all the emphasis on the powers of the Senate, of the President, of the Supreme Court? Everything was being done—as the fiery Patrick Henry was soon to cry out—*against* the "spirit of republicanism," *against* the "genius of democracy"!

The complaints of the three dissenters reached a crescendo during the final days of the Convention. They rose to explain why they could not sign the document. They foresaw a dangerous drift of the American Republic toward either monarchy or aristocracy. An all-powerful President or an arrogant Senate would crush the liberties of the people.

The following selection, containing these warnings, is from James Madison's *Debates in the Federal Convention of 1787* (first published 1900).

129

Mr. RANDOLPH declared, if no change should be made in this part of the plan [the method of ratification], he should be obliged to dissent from the whole of it. He had from the beginning he said been convinced that radical changes in the system of the Union were necessary. Under this conviction he had brought forward a set of republican propositions as the basis and outline of a reform. These Republican propositions had however, much to his regret, been widely . . . departed from.

In this state of things it was his idea . . . that the State Conventions should be at liberty to offer amendments to the plan; and that these should be submitted to a second General Convention, with full power to settle the Constitution finally.

A few days later George Mason asked why the Constitution did not include a Bill of Rights.

Colonel MASON . . . He wished the plan had been prefaced with a Bill of Rights, & would second a Motion if made for the purpose. It would give great quiet to the people; and with the aid of the State declarations [of rights], a bill might be prepared in a few hours. . . .

Mr. SHERMAN, was for securing the rights of the people where requisite. The State Declarations of Rights are not repealed by this Constitution; and being in force are sufficient.

On the next to last day of the Convention, the dissidents explained once more their objections to the Constitution.

130

Mr. RANDOLPH animadverting on the indefinite and dangerous power given by the Constitution to Congress . . . made a motion importing "that amendments to the plan might be offered by the State Conventions, which should be submitted to and finally decided on by another general Convention." Should this proposition be disregarded, it would he said be impossible for him to put his name to the instrument. . . .

Colonel MASON seconded & followed Mr. Randolph in animadversions on the dangerous power and structure of the Government, concluding that it would end either in monarchy, or a tyrannical aristocracy; which, he was in doubt, but one or other, he was sure. This Constitution had been formed without the knowledge or idea of the people. A second Convention will know more of the sense of the people, and be able to provide a system more consonant to it. . . .

Mr. PINCKNEY. . . . Nothing but confusion & contrariety could spring from the experiment [of asking the states for amendments]. The States will never agree in their plans, and the Deputies to a second Convention coming together under the discordant impressions of their Constituents, will never agree.

Conventions are serious things, and ought not to be repeated. He was not without objections as well as others to the plan. . . . But apprehending the danger of a general confusion, and an ultimate decision by the sword, he should give the plan his support.

Mr. GERRY, stated the objections which determined him to withhold his name from the Constitution [these included counting three-fifths of the black slaves "as if they were freemen" and Congress' power to set its own pay]. . . . He could however he said get over all these, if the rights of the Citizens were not rendered insecure first, by the general power of the Legislature to make what laws they may please . . . ; secondly, to raise armies and money without limit; thirdly, to establish a tribunal without juries [the federal judiciary]. . . . Under such a view of the Constitution, the best that could be done he conceived was to provide for a second general Convention.

BENJAMIN FRANKLIN'S COUNSEL

In spite of the grumblers, Benjamin Franklin's dream was coming true. After thirty-three years of turmoil, war, and revolution, the nation was to be offered a Constitution which *might* make possible the continental empire he had envisioned. But would the American people see with his eyes and believe with his faith? And what about the dissenting delegates?

Franklin sat down at his desk and wrote a short address to the Convention on its closing day, Monday, September 17. He invented a clever formula by which even the opponents of the Constitution could sign. They would sign simply as witnesses that it had been approved by all the *states* present—since voting was by states. And he urged all to lay aside their private doubts and sign as evidence of American unity and harmony. (Franklin himself had been troubled by the power given the President.)

The following selection is from Franklin's address, one of the most eloquent of his writings. Since the eighty-one-year-old Franklin was too weak to stand for long, the address was read aloud by his Pennsylvania colleague

James Wilson. The selection is from James Madison's *Debates in the Federal Convention of 1787* (first published 1900).

Doctor FRANKLIN rose with a speech in his hand, which he had reduced to writing for his own convenience, and which Mr. Wilson read in the words following.

"Mr. President

"I confess that there are several parts of this constitution which I do not at present approve, but I am not sure I shall never approve them: For having lived long, I have experienced many instances of being obliged by better information, or fuller consideration, to change opinions even on important subjects. . . . The older I grow, the more apt I am to doubt my own judgment, and to pay more respect to the judgment of others.

"Most men indeed as well as most sects in Religion, think themselves in possession of all truth. . . . But though many private persons think almost as highly of their infallibility as of that of their sect, few express it so naturally as a certain french lady, who in a dispute with her sister, said 'I don't know how it happens, Sister but I meet with no body but myself, that's always in the right.' . . .

"In these sentiments, Sir, I agree to this Constitution with all its faults, if they are such; because I think a general Government necessary for us, and there is no form of government but what may be a blessing to the people if well administered. . . . I doubt too whether any other Convention we can obtain, may be able to make a better Constitution. . . .

"Thus I consent, Sir, to this Constitution because I expect no better, and because I am not sure, that it is not the best. The opinions I have had of its errors, I sacrifice to the public good. I have never whispered a syllable of them abroad. . . . If every one of us in returning to our Constituents were to report the objections he has had to it . . . we might prevent its being generally received, and thereby lose all the salutary effects & great advantages resulting . . . among foreign Nations as well as among ourselves, from our real or apparent unanimity. . . . I hope therefore that for our own sakes . . . and for the sake of posterity, we shall act heartily and unanimously in recommending this Constitution. . . .

"On the whole, Sir, I cannot help expressing a wish that every member of the Convention who may still have objections to it, would with me, on this occasion doubt a little of his own infallibility, and . . . put his name to this instrument."

The three recalcitrant delegates were not persuaded by Dr. Franklin's stratagem. However, as the other delegates arose and came forward, one by one, to George Washington's desk to sign the parchment Constitution, Benjamin Franklin had the last word. The concluding passage from James Madison's *Debates in the Federal Convention of 1787* (first published 1900) narrates the incident.

Whilst the last members were signing it Doctor FRANKLIN looking towards the President's Chair, at the back of which a rising sun happened to be painted, observed to a few members near him, that Painters had found it difficult to distinguish in their art a rising from a setting sun. I have, said he, often and often in the course of the Session . . . looked at that behind the President without being able to tell whether it was rising or setting: But now at length I have the happiness to know that it is a rising and not a setting Sun.

The Constitution being signed by all the members except Mr. Randolph, Mr. Mason, and Mr. Gerry who declined giving it the sanction of their names, the Convention dissolved itself by an Adjournment sine die [permanent adjournment].

THE RIGHTS OF MAN

The Ratification of the Conventions of nine States, shall be sufficient for the Establishment of this Constitution between the States so ratifying the Same.

—The Constitution

CRITICS OF THE CONSTITUTION

The east room in the State House was now occupied by the Pennsylvania Assembly; the Convention stood adjourned. George Washington took up his quill pen and wrote a covering letter, then sent the Constitution to the Congress in New York. Delegates to the Convention who were also members of Congress prodded that slow-moving body to vote, September 28, 1787, to pass the Constitution along to the states. The people of each state prepared to elect conventions, to ratify or reject the new charter.

Then the battle began. The strategy of the opponents of the Constitution, the Antifederalists, was to delay the drive for quick ratification. They appealed to the fear of change, to the suspicions of backwoods debtors that the wealthy classes of the seaboard would cheat them, to state pride.

Since the Constitution promised to assume state debts, it did in some ways favor the creditor class. People would be taxed to pay off these debts to the individuals—often rich—who held government securities.

When Delaware ratified the Constitution on December 7, 1787, after only five days of debate in its convention, the Antifederalists cried that Delaware had "reaped the honor of having first surrendered the liberties of the people!"

Two of the three delegates who had refused to sign the Constitution became leaders of the Antifederalists. George Mason had left Philadelphia "in an exceeding ill humor"—because none of his protests had been heeded. Elbridge Gerry, the unpredictable merchant of Marblehead, declared that he could "never" accept the Constitution unless a second convention were summoned to improve it. "A Grumbletonian," a contemporary called Gerry—he was found "objecting to everything he did not propose."

But there was more than personality involved. On October 7, 1787, George Mason sent his neighbor George Washington a short paper containing his objections to the Constitution. Significantly, the paper begins with the words "There is no declaration of rights." This omission was nearly to prove the Achilles' heel of the Federalist cause.

It was in vain that the Federalists replied that these rights could be taken for granted, or that they were guaranteed in the state constitutions, or that the Constitution left all powers it did not name in the hands of the people. This would not satisfy the age of republicanism and the rights of man.

The following selection is from George Mason's "Objections to the Proposed Constitution" (from Jonathan Elliot, ed., *The Debates in the Several State Conventions on the Adoption of the Federal Constitution*).

There is no declaration of rights; and, the laws of the general government being paramount to [superior to] the laws and constitutions of the several states, the declarations of rights in the separate states are no security. . . .

In the House of Representatives there is not the substance, but the shadow only, of representation [*i.e.*, 30,000 constituents—as urged by Washington— are too many for just one representative]. . . .

The Senate have the power of altering all money bills, and . . . the salaries of the officers of their own appointment. . . . These, with their other great powers, (viz., their powers in the appointment of ambassadors, and all public officers, in making treaties, and in trying all impeachments); their influence upon, and connection with, the supreme executive . . . ; their duration of office . . . will . . . enable them to accomplish what usurpations they please upon the rights and liberties of the people.

The judiciary of the United States . . . [will] absorb and destroy the judiciaries of the several states. . . .

The President of the United States has no constitutional council [official advisers who might check his power]. . . . From this fatal defect . . . has arisen the improper power of the Senate in the appointment of the public officers. . . . Hence, also, sprang that unnecessary officer, the Vice-President, who, for want of other employment, is made president of the Senate. . . .

There is no declaration of any kind for preserving the liberty of the press, the trial by jury in civil cases, nor against the danger of standing armies in time of peace.

Early in 1788, Elbridge Gerry jotted down the arguments against the Constitution that he had been voicing in Massachusetts. This numbered list was published as a pamphlet "by a Columbian Patriot." It was one of the most complete, yet concise summaries of the Antifederalist case. Probably for that reason, it was reprinted in New York and widely distributed among the Antifederalists battling the Constitution there.

The following selection is from Elbridge Gerry's *Observations on the New Constitution* (1788).

[1.] The most sagacious advocates . . . have not . . . evinced the necessity of adopting this many headed monster [the Constitution]; of such motley mixture, that its enemies cannot trace a feature of Democratic or Republican extract; nor have its friends the courage to denominate a Monarchy, an Aristocracy, or an Oligarchy....

2. There is no security in the proffered system, either for the rights of conscience or the liberty of the Press....

3. There are no well defined limits of the Judiciary Powers, they seem to be left as a boundless ocean....

4. The Executive and the Legislative are so dangerously blended as to give just cause of alarm....

5. The abolition of trial by jury in civil causes....

6. Though it has been said by Mr. *Wilson* and many others, that a Standing Army is necessary for the dignity and safety of America, yet freedom revolts at the idea....

7. Notwithstanding the delusory promise to guarantee a Republican form of government to every State in the Union . . . there are no resources left for the support of internal [state] government, or the liquidation of the debts of the State....

8. As the new Congress are empowered to determine their own salaries, the requisitions for this purpose may not be very moderate....

9. There is no provision for a rotation, nor anything to prevent the perpetuity of office in the same hands for life; which by a little well timed bribery, will probably be done....

10. The inhabitants of the United States, are liable to be dragged from the vicinity of their own country, or state, to answer the litigious or unjust suit of an adversary, on the most distant borders of the Continent....

11. One Representative to thirty thousand inhabitants is a very inadequate representation....

12. . . . The circumscribing the votes to only ten

electors [of the President] in this State, and the same proportion in all the others, is nearly tantamount to the exclusion of the voice of the people in the choice of their first magistrate. . . .

13. A Senate chosen for six years will, in most instances, be an appointment for life. . . .

14. There is no provision by a bill of rights to guard against the dangerous encroachments of power. . . . The rights of individuals ought to be the primary object of all government, and cannot be too securely guarded by the most explicit declarations in their favor. . . .

15. The difficulty, if not impracticability, of exercising the . . . powers of government by a single legislature over an extent of territory that reaches from the Mississippi to the Western lakes, and from them to the Atlantic Ocean, is an insuperable objection to the adoption of the new system. . . .

16. . . . Not one legislature in the United States had the most distant idea when they first appointed members for a convention . . . that they would without any warrant from their constituents, presume on so bold and daring a stride, as ultimately to destroy the state governments, and offer a *consolidated system*. . . .

17. . . . The article which declares the ratification of nine states sufficient for the establishment of the new system . . . is a subversion of the union of Confederated States [in which a unanimous vote is required for any change]. . . .

18. The mode in which this constitution is recommended to the people to judge without either the advice of Congress, or the legislatures of the several states is very reprehensible—it is an attempt to force it upon them before it could be thoroughly understood.

A SCOTS LAWYER TO THE RESCUE

The reasoned objections of Mason and Gerry were buttressed by more emotional arguments. Richard Henry Lee of Virginia warned that the Constitution would "produce a coalition of monarchy men, military men, aristocrats and drones." A Baptist preacher in North Carolina thought the proposed seat of government—the future District of Columbia—would be "walled in or fortified"; from it "an army of 50,000 or perhaps 100,000 men . . . will sally forth and enslave the people."

"James the Caledonian"—sturdy James Wilson of Pennsylvania—replied to the rational arguments of the Antifederalists. Speaking before the Pennsylvania legislature, October 9, 1787, he discussed the absence of a bill of rights. He tried to reassure the Antifederalists that the President had not been given too much power; that a "baneful aristocracy" would not be created in the Senate; that direct taxation of the people by the federal government was necessary and was not dangerous; that jury trials could be held in civil (*i.e.*, property) cases.

When the ratifying convention for Pennsylvania met in late November and early December, Wilson repeated his arguments. The Federalists had won a majority of the delegates by a high-pressure campaign. In the convention they continued their powerhouse tactics and secured the ratification of the Constitution on December 12, 1787.

But in the backcountry this outcome was not popular. Wilson was denounced for pride—though a friendly newspaper declared that a man who wore spectacles had to hold his head high to keep them from slipping off his nose. In Carlisle, where Wilson had once been a leading lawyer, he was burnt in effigy!

The following selection is from James Wilson's "Defense of the Constitution, in the State House of Pennsylvania" (from John B. McMaster and F. D. Stone, eds., *Pennsylvania and the Federal Constitution, 1787–1788*).

When the people established the powers of legislation under their separate [state] governments, they invested their representatives with every right and authority which they did not in explicit terms reserve. . . . But in delegating federal powers, another criterion was necessarily introduced, and the congressional power is to be collected [understood], not from tacit implication, but from the positive grant [of powers] expressed in the instrument of the union [*i.e.* the Constitution]. Hence . . . everything which is not given [in the Constitution] is reserved.

This distinction . . . will furnish an answer to those who think the omission of a bill of rights a defect in the proposed constitution; for it would have been superfluous . . . to have stipulated with a federal body of our own creation, that we should enjoy those privileges of which we are not divested. . . . For instance, the liberty of the press . . .—what control can proceed from the Federal government to shackle or destroy that sacred palladium of national freedom? If, indeed, a power similar to that which has been granted for the regulation of commerce had been granted to regulate literary publications, it would have been . . . necessary to stipulate that the liberty of the press should be preserved. . . .

Perhaps there never was a charge made with less reasons than that which predicts the institution of a baneful aristocracy in the federal Senate. This body branches into two characteristics, the one legislative and the other executive. In its legislative character it can effect no purpose, without the co-operation of the House of Representatives, and in its executive character it can accomplish no object without the concurrence of the President. Thus fettered, I do not know any act which the Senate can of itself perform, and such dependence necessarily precludes every idea of influence and superiority. . . .

The power of direct taxation has likewise been treated as an improper delegation to the federal government; but when we consider it as the duty of that body to provide for the national safety, to support the dignity of the union, and to discharge the debts contracted upon the collected faith of the States for their common benefit, it must be acknowledged that [the federal government] . . . ought . . . to possess every means requisite for a faithful performance of their trust. . . .

If there are errors, it should be remembered that the seeds of reformation are sown in the work itself, and the concurrence of two-thirds of the Congress may at any time introduce alterations and amendments. Regarding it, then, in every point of view . . . I am bold to assert that it is the best form of government which has ever been offered to the world.

ADVANTAGES OF A GREAT REPUBLIC

The most philosophical defense of the Constitution was the work of Alexander Hamilton, James Madison, and John Jay. From October, 1787, through 1788 their *Federalist* essays appeared in various New York newspapers. Each essay was like a commentator's column in one of today's newspapers. Each essay analyzed and refuted some argument against the new plan of government.

James Madison, for example, took up Montesquieu's objection that a republic must "have only a small territory; otherwise it cannot long subsist" and answered it. Madison found that a large republic was not only feasible but would offer special safeguards against "factions"— that is, against pressure groups or lobbies.

The *Federalist* became a classic; it is considered the most important single interpretation of the Constitution and has often been cited by the Supreme Court in its decisions.

The following selection is from two of Madison's essays in the *Federalist* (1787–88).

The error which limits republican government to a narrow district has been . . . refuted in preceding papers. I remark here only that it seems to owe its rise and prevalence chiefly to the confounding of a republic with a democracy, applying to the former reasonings drawn from the nature of the latter. The true distinction between these forms . . . is, that in a democracy, the people meet and exercise the government in person; in a republic, they assemble and administer it by their representatives and agents. A democracy, consequently, will be confined to a small spot. A republic may be extended over a large region. . . .

As the natural limit of a democracy is that distance from the central point which will just permit the most remote citizens to assemble as often as their public functions demand . . . so the natural limit of a republic is that distance from the centre which will barely allow the representatives to meet as often as may be necessary for the administration of public affairs.

Can it be said that the limits of the United States exceed this distance? It will not be said by those who recollect that the Atlantic coast is the longest side of the Union, that during the term of thirteen years, the representatives of the States have been almost continually assembled, and that the members from the most distant States are not chargeable with greater intermissions of attendance than those from the States in the neighborhood of Congress. . . .

[We may add] that the intercourse throughout the Union will be facilitated by new improvements. Roads will everywhere be shortened, and kept in better order; accommodations for travellers will be multiplied and meliorated [improved]; an interior navigation on our eastern side will be opened throughout, or nearly throughout, . . . the thirteen States. The communication between the Western and Atlantic districts, and between different parts of each, will be rendered more and more easy by . . . numerous canals.

Among the numerous advantages promised by a well-constructed Union, none deserves to be more accurately developed than its tendency to break and control the violence of faction. . . .

By a faction, I understand a number of citizens, whether amounting to a majority or minority of the whole, who are united and actuated by some common impulse of passion, or of interest, adverse to the rights of other citizens, or to the permanent and aggregated interests of the community. . . .

A pure democracy . . . can admit of no cure for the mischiefs of faction. A common passion or interest will . . . be felt by a majority of the whole; a communication and concert [uniting] result from the form of government itself; and there is nothing to check the inducements to sacrifice the weaker party or an obnoxious individual. . . .

A republic . . . opens a different prospect, and promises the cure for which we are seeking. . . .

The two great points of difference between a democracy and a republic are: first, the delegation of the government, in the latter, to a small number of citizens elected by the rest; secondly, the greater number of citizens, and greater sphere of country, over which the latter may be extended.

The effect of the first difference is . . . to refine and enlarge the public views, by passing them through the medium of a chosen body of citizens, whose wisdom may best discern the true interest of their country. . . . It may well happen that the public voice, pronounced by the representatives of the people, will be more consonant to the public good than if pronounced by the people themselves. . . .

[The effect of the second difference is that] you take in a greater variety of parties and interests; you make it less probable that a majority of the whole will have a common motive to invade the rights of other citizens; or . . . it will be more difficult [for them] . . . to act in unison with each other. . . .

The influence of factious leaders may kindle a flame within their particular States, but will be unable to spread a general conflagration through the other States. A religious sect may degenerate into a political faction in a part of the Confederacy; but the variety of sects dispersed over the entire face of it must secure the national councils against any danger from that source. A rage for paper money, for an abolition of debts, for an equal division of property, or for any other improper or wicked project, will be less apt to pervade the whole body of the Union than a particular member of it. . . .

In the extent and proper structure of the Union, therefore, we behold a republican remedy for the diseases most incident to republican government.

PATRICK HENRY FIRES A BROADSIDE

Because they had something positive to offer, the Federalists gained an early momentum. They needed ratification by nine states out of thirteen. By mid-January, 1788, they had won in Delaware, New Jersey, Georgia, Connecticut, and Pennsylvania.

Four of these five, however, were small states. For the Union to succeed, not only Pennsylvania but also Massachusetts, New York, and Virginia had to come in. In the late winter and spring of 1788 the Antifederalists redoubled their efforts in these states.

"To say that a bad government must be established for fear of anarchy is really saying that we should kill ourselves for fear of dying!" protested Richard Henry Lee.

They failed in Massachusetts, which ratified the Constitution on February 6, 1788. Here even the old-fashioned Sam Adams was converted when a meeting of mechanics led by Paul Revere backed the new charter. But then came the most crucial struggle of all, in the most influential state, Virginia.

Virginia Federalists included James Madison, Edmund Pendleton, George Wythe, and Edmund Randolph, the handsome governor who had refused to sign the Constitution but now changed his mind again. But the Antifederalist appeared still more formidable, with George Mason, James Monroe, William Grayson, Richard Henry Lee—and Patrick Henry.

Patrick Henry, the gaunt, organ-voiced backwoodsman, spoke once more for "liberty," as he had in his great speeches of 1775. When he had cried in the crowded Richmond church on the eve of the Revolution, "Give me liberty or—give me death!"—striking himself over the heart with his clenched right hand as though with a dagger—he had been "like a Roman Senator defying Caesar," said one witness. Another young Virginian, hearing those burning words, begged his friends to carry his body back, when he died, and bury it on that spot.

Now Patrick Henry spoke for "liberty" meaning states' rights; "liberty" for local government, "liberty" for the individualistic backwoods to be free of the nuisance or oppression of a distant central government. He declaimed against "two sets of tax-gatherers." He compared "the tyranny of Philadelphia" to "the tyranny of George III."

His deep voice made the chandeliers ring, and men for the moment forgot the disorder under the Articles of Confederation. They forgot that the Antifederalists had been unable to agree on any alternative to the Constitution. They felt transported back to the times of the Revolution—to the glorious early days of "republicanism," "self-rule," and "independence."

The following selection includes passages from several of Patrick Henry's speeches made in the Virginia convention, June 2–25, 1788 (from Jonathan Elliot, ed., *The Debates in the Several State Conventions*).

What right had they to say, *We, the people*? . . . Who authorized them to speak the language of, *We, the people*, instead of, *We, the states*? States are the characteristics and the soul of a confederation. . . .

Have they said, We, the states? Have they made a proposal of a compact between states? If they had, this would be a confederation. It is otherwise most clearly a consolidated government. . . . I need not take much pains to show that the principles of this system are extremely pernicious, impolitic, and dangerous. . . . It is not a democracy, wherein the people retain all their rights securely. . . .

The rights of conscience, trial by jury, liberty of the press, all your immunities and franchises, all pretensions to human rights and privileges, are rendered insecure, if not lost, by this change. . . . Is this tame relinquishment of rights worthy of freemen? . . . It is said eight states have adopted this plan. I declare that if twelve states and a half had adopted it, I would, with manly firmness, and in spite of an erring world, reject it. You are not to inquire how your trade may be increased, nor how you are to become a great and powerful people, but how your liberties can be secured; for liberty ought to be the direct end of your government. . . .

Will the abandonment of your most sacred rights tend to the security of your liberty? Liberty, the greatest of all earthly blessings—give us that precious jewel, and you may take every thing else! But I am fearful I have lived long enough to become an old-fashioned fellow. Perhaps an invincible attachment to the dearest rights of man may, in these refined, enlightened days, be deemed old-fashioned; if so, I am contented to be so. . . .

If we admit this consolidated government, it will be because we like a great, splendid one. Some way or other we must be a great and mighty empire; we must have an army, and a navy, and a number of things. When the American spirit was in its youth, the language of America was different: liberty, sir, was then the primary object. . . . But now, sir, the American spirit, assisted by the ropes and chains of consolidation, is about to convert this country into a powerful and mighty empire. If you make the citizens of this country agree to become the subjects of one great consolidated empire of America, your government will not have sufficient energy to keep them together. Such a government is incompatible with the genius of republicanism. . . .

Beside the expenses of maintaining the Senate and other house in as much splendor as they please, there is to be a great and mighty President, with very extensive powers—the powers of a king. He is to be supported in extravagant magnificence; so that the whole of our property may be taken by this American government, by laying what taxes they please, giving themselves what salaries they please, and suspending our laws at their pleasure. . . . Your President may easily become king. . . .

In this scheme of energetic government, the people will find two sets of tax-gatherers—the state and the federal sheriffs. This, it seems to me, will produce such dreadful oppression as the people cannot possibly bear. The federal sheriff may commit what oppression, make what distresses, he pleases, and ruin you with impunity; for how are you to tie his hands? . . . Thousands of your people will be most shamefully robbed.

THE FEDERALISTS COUNTERATTACK

Patrick Henry's assault was formidable. When he thundered a warning against the "chains of consolidation," one delegate "involuntarily felt his wrists to assure himself that the fetters were not already pressing his flesh." Henry had been summoning his supporters from the ends of the Old Dominion, whose territory still included Kentucky. Fourteen Kentuckians sat in the rear of the Richmond Academy hall, waiting to vote against ratification. Since they had traveled through Indian country, they wore their pistols as their sides!

The Federalists could not match Patrick Henry's oratory, so they answered him not with emotion but with reason. Governor Randolph asserted the Federalists' faith in the people, who would both pass on the Constitution and elect the new President. Madison, coolly reading his notes out of the bottom of his cocked hat, agreed with Henry's attack on imperialism, but he reminded Henry of the chaos that foreign relations had fallen into under the Articles of Confederation.

It is true that the Federalists were not old-fashioned republicans (Old Whigs) who emphasized local government. But they *were* republicans. They accepted Locke's doctrine of the sovereignty of the people; they championed the separation of powers and limitations on the central government almost as fervently as Patrick Henry did. What they wanted was a balance between local government and a central government strong enough to give the people greater security than town meetings or state legislatures could provide.

In some ways the Federalists were less cynical, more trusting in the people, than the people's professed champions. The Antifederalists tended to argue that *no* government could be trusted, that *every* official, and even "the people" who elected him, would become corrupt.

The following selection is from the rebuttal of Patrick Henry by Edmund Randolph. Randolph had refused to sign the Constitution in Philadelphia, partly because he feared a reaction threatening his political base in Virginia, from Henry and his friends. Now his desire for a strong Union made him shift again, and he brought a large popular following with him. (The selection is from Jonathan Elliot, ed., *The Debates in the Several State Conventions.*)

The gentleman [Patrick Henry] . . . inquires why we assumed the language of "We, the people." I ask Why not? The government is for the people. . . . What harm is there in consulting the people on the construction of a government by which they are to be bound? Is it unfair? Is it unjust? If the government is to be binding on the people, are not the people the proper persons to examine its merits or defects? . . .

Let us consider whether the federal executive [the President] be wisely constructed. . . . It cannot be objected to the federal executive that the power is executed by one man. All the enlightened part of mankind agree that the superior dispatch, secrecy, and energy, with which one man can act, render it more politic to vest the power of executing the laws in one man than in any number of men.

How is the President elected? By the people—on the same day throughout the United States—by those whom the people please [the electors]. There can be no concert [agreement or conspiracy] between the electors. The votes are sent sealed to Congress.

What are his powers? To see the laws executed. Every executive in America has that power. He is also to command the army: this power also is enjoyed by the executives of the different states. He can handle no part of the public money except what is given him by law. At the end of four years, he may be turned out of office. If he misbehaves he may be impeached, and in this case he will never be reelected. I cannot conceive how his powers can be called formidable. Both houses are a check upon him. He can do no important act without the concurrence of the Senate. . . .

In England, the king declares war. In America, Congress must be consulted. In England, Parliament gives money. In America, Congress does it. There are consequently more powers in the hands of the people, and greater checks upon the executive here, than in England. . . .

It is also objected that the trial by jury, the writ of *habeas corpus*, and the liberty of the press are insecure. But I contend that the *habeas corpus* is at least on as secure and good a footing as it is in England. In that country, it depends on the will of the legislature. That privilege is secured here by the Constitution, and is only to be suspended in cases of extreme emergency. Is this not a fair footing? . . . Why distrust ourselves?

The liberty of the press is supposed to be in danger. If this were the case, it would produce extreme repugnancy in my mind. If it ever will be suppressed in this country, the liberty of the people will not be far from being sacrificed. Where is the danger of it? He [Patrick Henry] says that every power is given to the general government that is not reserved to the states. Pardon me if I say the reverse . . . is true. I defy any one to prove the contrary. Every power not given it [the federal government] by this system is left with the states. This being the principle, from what part of the Constitution can the liberty of the press be said to be in danger?

The following selection is from the rebuttal of Patrick Henry by James Madison (from Jonathan Elliot, ed., *The Debates in the Several State Conventions*).

I agree with the honorable gentleman (Mr. Henry) that national splendor and glory are not our objects; but does he distinguish between what will render us secure and happy at home, and what will render us respectable abroad? If we be free and happy at home, we shall be respectable abroad.

The Confederation is so notoriously feeble, that foreign nations are unwilling to form any treaties with us; they are apprized that our general government cannot perform any of its engagements, but that they may be violated at pleasure by any of the states. Our violation of treaties already entered into proves this truth unequivocally. No nation will, therefore, make any stipulations with Congress, conceding any advantages of importance to us: they will be the more averse to entering into engagements with us, as the imbecility [weakness] of our government enables them to derive many advantages from our trade, without granting us any return.

But were this country united by proper bands, in addition to other great advantages, we could form very beneficial treaties with foreign states. But this can never happen without a change in our system.

ALLIGATORS AND INDIANS

The speeches in the Virginia convention were impassioned but courteous—and, occasionally, humorous. William Grayson, a dedicated Antifederalist, thought the Federalist argument of "The Constitution—or anarchy!" slightly exaggerated. This skeptic, who had opposed the Constitution in Congress, now parodied the dire warnings of those who supported it. The following selection is from Grayson's speech (from Jonathan Elliot, ed., *The Debates in the Several State Conventions*).

We are now told by the honorable gentleman [Governor Randolph] that we shall have wars and rumors of wars, that every calamity is to attend us, and that we shall be ruined and disunited forever, unless we adopt this Constitution. Pennsylvania and Maryland are to fall upon us from the north, like the

Goths and Vandals of old; the Algerines [pirates of Algiers], whose flat-sided vessels never came farther than Madeira, are to fill the Chesapeake with mighty fleets, and to attack us on our front; the Indians are to invade us with numerous armies on our rear, in order to convert our cleared lands into hunting-grounds; and the Carolinians, from the south, (mounted on alligators, I presume,) are to come and destroy our cornfields, and eat up our little children!

A NAGGING QUESTION

The champions of the Constitution could brush off mocking attacks like William Grayson's. But one nagging question they could not answer.

Why had they not included a bill of rights in the Constitution? Why did not the charter of the Republic, like the Declaration of Independence, proclaim the inalienable liberties of the individual?

"I will now add what I do not like [about the Constitution]," Thomas Jefferson wrote Madison from France. "First, the omission of a bill of rights."

All the precise, legalistic explanations of James Madison and James Wilson would not satisfy the questioners. Eighteenth-century republicanism did not have as its goal empire building, but a new world of liberty, fraternity, and equality for all.

When Massachusetts ratified the Constitution in February, 1788, it tacked on nine recommended amendments. These established a trend which South Carolina (May 28, 1788) and New Hampshire (June 21, 1788) followed. Toward the end of the debates in the Virginia convention, when eight states had ratified and New Hampshire was poised to vote, crusty George Mason raised the question again. He "still thought that there ought to be . . . a bill of rights."

James Madison and the other managers of the Federalists' campaign were forced to yield. They agreed to accept ratification with suggested amendments. Then at last, four days after New Hampshire voted, the Virginia convention ratified the Constitution, 89–79. But the delegates added a declaration of rights and no fewer than twenty other amendments designed to safeguard the Western tradition of personal freedom.

THE ANCIENT TRADITION

Where did this idea of personal freedom come from? Roman law stated that governments derive their right to rule from the people. Roman writers explained that the people had granted the right to rule to Augustus *and* his successors—once for all.

But during the Middle Ages the scholars of Western Europe interpreted the doctrine to mean that each ruler, in turn, had to govern for the welfare of his people. If he misgoverned, the people could assert their sovereignty—take back the right to rule—by rebelling against him. As St. Thomas Aquinas put it, revolt against a tyrant is no sin. For this teaching, St. Thomas Aquinas has been called the first Whig.

Medieval scholars also developed a doctrine of the supremacy of law. Rulers, as well as their people, are subject to the law. For the Middle Ages, at least in theory, there could be no such thing as absolute rule—a king above or beyond the law.

In 1215 the English barons revolted against the arbitrary rule of King John and forced him to sign the Magna Carta. This "Great Charter," written on a huge parchment 18¼ inches long by 17¾ inches wide, establishes the supremacy of law. One famous article states that no free man—later changed to read "no man of whatever estate or condition he may be"—may be deprived of life or property without due process. The English even derive the right to a jury trial from this article:

"39. No free man shall be taken or imprisoned or disseised [dispossessed] or outlawed or exiled or in any way ruined, nor will we go or send against him, except by the lawful judgement of his peers or by the law of the land."

Later, during the Renaissance (1450–1625), an attempt was made to establish absolute government through the doctrine of the divine right of kings. Kings were said to derive their right to rule from God, not from the people. Disobedience to a ruler under *any* circumstances was sinful. The ruler was responsible to God, not to his subjects.

English Whigs did not accept this defense of the Stuart monarchy. The Whigs were a middle-class party that supported the rights of Parliament. They revolted in 1642 and again in 1688. In 1688 they won a lasting victory by not only banishing James II but also making Parliament supreme over the new king. In 1689 Parliament passed a Bill of Rights justifying the rebellion against James II and stating a number of the traditional rights Americans would claim a century later.

The following selection is from the English Bill of Rights of 1689.

1. That the pretended power of suspending of laws, or the execution of laws, by regal authority, without consent of Parliament, is illegal.

5. That it is the right of the subjects to petition

the King, and all commitments and prosecutions for such petitioning are illegal.

6. That the raising or keeping a standing army within the kingdom in time of peace, unless it be with consent of Parliament, is against law.

8. That election of members of Parliament ought to be free.

9. That the freedom of speech, and debates or proceedings in Parliament, ought not to be impeached or questioned in any court or place out of Parliament.

10. That excessive bail ought not to be required, nor excessive fines imposed; nor cruel and unusual punishments inflicted.

THE VIRGINIA DECLARATION OF RIGHTS

On June 12, 1776, the Virginia convention had adopted the first American Declaration of Rights. Typical of "the spirit of defiance shown in the Revolutionary era," it was largely the work of George Mason.

The "squire of Gunston Hall," with his shock of white hair and snapping black eyes, himself typified an eighteenth-century elitist approach. It is ironical that this outspoken champion of liberty was also the owner of 300 slaves. He was, however, a leader of Southern opposition to further importation of slaves and a spokesman for the gradual abolition of the institution.

The Virginia Declaration of Rights of 1776 is the chief link between the English Bill of Rights of 1689 and the Bill of Rights in the Constitution. A number of its articles, slightly changed, were to reappear among the first ten amendments.

The following selection is from the Virginia Declaration of Rights (from Mabel Hill, *Liberty Documents*).

I. That all men are by nature equally free and independent, and have certain inherent rights . . . namely, the enjoyment of life and liberty with the means of acquiring and possessing property, and pursuing and obtaining happiness and safety.

II. That all power is vested in, and consequently derived from, the people; that magistrates are their trustees and servants, and at all times amenable [responsible] to them.

III. . . . that, when a government shall be found inadequate . . . a majority of the community hath an indubitable, unalienable and indefeasible right to reform, alter or abolish it. . . .

V. That the legislative, executive and judicial powers should be separate. . . .

VI. That all elections ought to be free. . . .

VII. That all power of suspending laws, or the execution of laws, by an authority, without consent of the representatives of the people . . . ought not to be exercised.

VIII. That in all capital or criminal prosecutions, a man hath a right to demand the cause and nature of his accusation, to be confronted with the accusers and witnesses, to call for evidence in his favour, and to a speedy trial by an impartial jury of twelve men of his vicinage [district], without whose unanimous consent he cannot be found guilty. . . .

IX. That excessive bail ought not to be required, nor excessive fines imposed, nor cruel and unusual punishments inflicted.

XI. That in controversies respecting property, and in suits between man and man, the ancient trial by jury of twelve men is preferable to any other. . . .

XII. That the freedom of the press is one of the great bulwarks of liberty, and can never be restrained but by despotic governments.

XVI. That religion . . . can be directed only by reason and conviction, not by force or violence; and therefore all men are equally entitled to the free exercise of religion, according to the dictates of conscience.

"THE BLESSINGS OF LIBERTY"

After New Hampshire (June 21) and Virginia (June 25) had ratified the Constitution, an inspired Alexander Hamilton turned the tide against the Antifederalists who were dominant in his state. The New York convention was persuaded by Hamilton to ratify the plan, July 26.

That left two states undecided. North Carolina voted no in August, 1788, but changed its mind a year later; Rhode Island straggled into the Union in May, 1790.

But the demand for a bill of rights proved irresistible. James Madison campaigned on a promise to introduce such a bill in Congress. When he was elected to the House of Representatives, he kept his promise. In March, 1789, Congress sent twelve proposed amendments to the states. Two nonessential ones—setting Congressional salaries and going into detail about how many people a Congressman's district should include—were dropped. The other ten became part of the Constitution on December 15, 1791.

These ten amendments are the culmination of the tradition which had originated in the Middle Ages and had been carried on by the English-speaking forebears of the colonists. The amendments completed the Constitution, just as the spire crowns a cathedral. Indeed, when the Constitution is mentioned today, the odds are that the speaker is thinking primarily of this Bill of Rights, along with the "We the People" preamble. These join the Constitution to the Declaration of Independence as the two great American documents proclaiming "the Blessings of Liberty."

EPILOGUE

On July 4, 1788, the staid city of Philadelphia awoke to a joyous peal of church bells and the boom of ship's cannon. It was the day chosen for the grand procession to celebrate the ratification of the Constitution.

Along the waterfront, ten ships were spread like a file of soldiers, each at its wharf, each with a white pennant fluttering from its masthead. Inscribed in gold letters on the pennants were the names of the states. *New Hampshire* for the first ship . . . then *Massachusetts . . . Connecticut . . . New Jersey . . . Pennsylvania . . . Delaware . . . Maryland . . . Virginia . . . South Carolina . . . Georgia . . .* the states of the new nation.

By nine thirty the parade was under way. Light dragoons, clad in blue coats edged with red, deftly managed their spirited horses in front. A horseman followed, carrying a staff twined with olive and laurel. Then came a band, then a float in the shape of a bright blue eagle, with thirteen stars emblazoned on its breast. Consuls from foreign nations occupied another float. In another sat a citizen and an Indian chief, the chief wearing scarlet and white plumes and extending a peace pipe to his comrade.

The climax was the float for the Grand Federal Edifice. The Edifice was a magnificent temple, with a dome supported by thirteen columns. Three of the columns, representing states which had not yet ratified, were unfinished. Ten white horses drew the Edifice. A statue of Plenty stood above the dome, with a slogan lettered around its pedestal: "In Union the Fabric stands firm."

And behind came, on foot, marching, architects and

carpenters; sawmakers and file cutters; brickmakers and clockmakers; ribbon weavers; saddlers; boat builders, sailmakers and ship joiners; blacksmiths and coachmakers; brewers and bakers; all the clergy "united in charity and brotherly love"—all marching to celebrate and, at the end, to toast "The people of the United States" and "The Whole Family of Mankind."

It was a grand and glorious Fourth. What it hailed, the Constitution of 1787, did indeed, as its framers hoped, mark a new beginning. The ideas of independence and republicanism, which had flamed forth in 1776, were now reinforced by the bond of unity, of true nationhood. These ideas would endure and would influence liberation movements in Europe and South America—even in distant Asia and Africa—for generations to come.

And the Constitution, as now ratified by "the people of the United States of America," was to prove both long-lived and adaptable. It would be reinterpreted by the Supreme Court, "a kind of Constitutional Convention in continuous session." It would be amended by Congress and the states. But both the interpretations and the amendments would keep the nation on the course plotted in 1787—toward the destiny of a community of free men.

Four periods have been distinguished in the history of Supreme Court rulings about the Constitution. In the first, Chief Justice John Marshall (in office 1801–1835), a firm believer in national sovereignty, defended the central government against the states. In the second, however, Chief Justice Roger Taney (in office 1836–1864) supported the states and wrote a crucial decision propping up slavery. Even after the Civil War had settled the question of the supremacy of the national government, the Court, in a third period lasting from 1865 to 1936, continued to incline toward the states and, often, to place property rights ahead of human rights. But in the fourth period, from the Roosevelt court of 1937 to the present, the Justices have given a new emphasis to human rights.

More important than alternating interpretations have been the handful of amendments. Unlike many state constitutions, the Constitution of 1787 has not been buried beneath innumerable wordy amendments. Counting the first ten amendments—the Bill of Rights of 1791—as part of the original document, there have only been a baker's dozen since.

The Eleventh and Twelfth Amendments remedied actual defects in the operation of the Constitution. The Thirteenth, Fourteenth, and Fifteenth are the Civil War amendments, freeing the black and guaranteeing—as much as law can—his possession of full civil rights. Then came a group of twentieth-century political reforms—the income tax (Sixteenth), the popular election of Senators (Seventeenth), woman's right to vote (Nineteenth), the doing away with lame duck sessions of Congress (Twentieth), the limitation of a President to two terms in office (Twenty-second), the right of District of Columbia residents to vote in Presidential elections (Twenty-third), and the abolition of the poll tax (Twenty-fourth).

Looking at the amendments more closely, we observe that the Eleventh prohibits individuals from suing a state. The Twelfth provides for the Presidential electors to vote for the President on one ballot, and for the Vice President on another, separate ballot—so that both President and Vice President will be members of the same political party. Before 1804, the Vice President was simply the runner-up in the balloting for President. Thus he might belong to an opposing political party.

Had the Convention at Philadelphia truly formed a nation in place of the old league of sovereign states? When Chief Justice Roger Taney gave his decision in the Dred Scott case (1857), the issue seemed in doubt. He ruled that Congress could not prohibit slavery in territory it controlled, that state laws decide the fate of any slave claiming freedom, and that a black slave or descendant of slaves could not be a citizen of the United States.

The American people overruled the Chief Justice. Between 1865 and 1870, after the gray tide of rebellion had been turned back at Gettysburg, the Thirteenth, Fourteenth, and Fifteenth Amendments were ratified. The Thirteenth declares: "Neither slavery nor involuntary servitude . . . shall exist within the United States." The Fourteenth declares: "No State shall . . . deprive any person of life, liberty, or property, without due process of law; nor deny to any person . . . the equal protection of the laws." The Fifteenth states: "The right of citizens of the United States to vote shall not be denied or abridged . . . on account of race, color, or previous condition of servitude." The Fourteenth Amendment was the basis of the 1954 Supreme Court decision striking down segregated schools. This amendment demands that states observe the Bill of Rights (especially the Fifth Amendment) and thus strengthens the liberties not only of blacks but of all citizens.

The twentieth-century political reforms achieved through the amendments are self-explanatory. One attempted social reform failed, however. This was the prohibition of the sale of alcoholic beverages by the Eighteenth Amendment. People did not obey the law, organized crime moved in, and as a result Americans, by the Twenty-first Amendment, repealed the Eighteenth.

That the Constitution is indeed a living document was shown dramatically in 1973. At that time a Senate committee investigating the Watergate scandal—the break-in at the headquarters of the Democratic National Committee —issued a subpoena to President Richard Nixon. The committee demanded that he surrender to it tape recordings of conversations between himself and his assistants which might help the committee decide on the truthfulness of certain witnesses. The President refused, and thus provoked a "Constitutional crisis."

The President claimed that the Constitutional doctrine of "separation of powers"—the independence of each of the three branches of government (Executive, Congress, Federal Courts)—gave him the right to keep these conversations private if he so desired. The Senate committee replied that since the tapes might contain evidence of crimes, the Executive could not place himself above the law by withholding them; that would be obstruction of justice. Earlier confrontations provided no clear precedents, and the issue was taken to the courts for settlement.

Historians pointed out that earlier confrontations, such as that between Thomas Jefferson and Chief Justice John Marshall or that between Woodrow Wilson and another Senate committee, offered no clear precedent. The issue was taken to the courts for settlement.

So this vital Constitution, which is continually reexamined and cited today, approaches its two hundredth birthday. It has been amended to cleanse away the stain of slavery (the word the Convention could not bring itself to use) and to increase the people's participation in government; it has been reinterpreted to broaden the liberties of the individual. But it is basically the same instrument the indefatigable Madison labored to bring forth under the calm gaze of the blue-coated general on the platform in the Philadelphia State House. It is the charter of a nation in which the common man, relieved of the burden of feudal overlords, can enjoy his God-given heritage of life, liberty, and the pursuit of happiness.

It underwrites an open society, the Heavenly City of ancient philosophers brought down to earth. It assumes, in the people, a willingness to work hard, to take part in political processes, and to respect the rights of others.

Thus the Constitution offers the individual a challenge

today, the same challenge its framers met. That is, to be the citizen of a nation founded not on loyalty to a region, a religious sect, or an ethnic group, but on an abstract ideal of liberty and justice for men of every race and every creed. It aims at unity without destroying diversity. *E pluribus unum*, says the Great Seal of the United States: from many cultures one free republic.

A TIMETABLE OF EVENTS

June–July, 1754. The Albany Congress adopts a plan of union devised by Benjamin Franklin, but the colonial assemblies later reject it.

September 12–18, 1759. Quebec, the bastion of French Canada, falls to the British forces commanded by James Wolfe.

February 10, 1763. By the Treaty of Paris, France cedes Canada to Great Britain.

July 4, 1776. The Second Continental Congress issues the Declaration of Independence.

March 1, 1781. The Articles of Confederation, having been ratified by all thirteen states, go into effect.

February 3, 1783. The Peace of Paris recognizes American independence and establishes the boundaries of the new nation.

September, 1786. The Annapolis Convention is persuaded by Alexander Hamilton and James Madison to recommend that a convention be held in Philadelphia to revise the Articles of Confederation.

September, 1786–February, 1787. The debt-ridden farmers of western Massachusetts unite under Captain Daniel Shays and rebel against their state.

February 21, 1787. Congress asks the states to send delegates to a convention to be held in Philadelphia, meeting the second Monday in May, to revise the Articles of Confederation.

May 14, 1787. Delegates from only two states, Pennsylvania and Virginia, appear for the scheduled first session of the Constitutional Convention; they adjourn to await late arrivals.

May 25, 1787. The first session of the Constitutional Convention is held with nine states represented; George Washington is the unanimous choice for president of the Convention.

May 29, 1787. The Virginia Plan, outlining a strong, "energetic" government and reflecting the ideas of James Madison, is presented by Edmund Randolph.

June 15, 1787. The New Jersey Plan, providing for only minor changes in the Articles of Confederation and safeguarding the sovereignty of the states, is presented by William Paterson.

June 19, 1787. The delegates vote to reject the New Jersey Plan and continue their discussion of the Virginia Plan.

June 28, 1787. As the power struggle between large and small states becomes more bitter, Benjamin Franklin proposes opening each session with a prayer.

July 2, 1787. The delegates are deadlocked over how many votes each state should have in the Senate and are "on the verge of dissolution"; they appoint a committee to seek a solution.

July 10, 1787. New York's states' right delegates, John Lansing and Robert Yates, leave the Convention in protest against the nationalists.

July 13, 1787. Congress passes the Northwest Ordinance, which provides for the organization of the territory north of the Ohio River—the most important law made under the Confederation.

July 16, 1787. By the narrow margin of one state, the Convention votes to accept the "Great Compromise"—equal representation of states in the Senate, proportional representation in the House. The large states complain, and the small states offer to end the Convention.

July 17–26, 1787. The delegates complete their discussion of the resolutions of the Virginia Plan.

July 26, 1787. The Convention adjourns until August 6 to allow time for a Committee of Detail to draw up a rough draft of the Constitution, based on the Virginia Plan as amended.

July 27–August 5, 1787. The delegates entertain themselves in or around Philadelphia or make short visits to their homes; George Washington goes fishing near Valley Forge.

August 6–September 8, 1787. The delegates consider the rough draft of the Constitution, article by article.

August 29, 1787. Northern and Southern states compromise their quarrel about the slave trade by allowing the trade to continue until 1800 (later changed to 1808).

September 6, 1787. A complicated plan for electing a President, arranged by a Committee on Postponed Matters, is accepted by the Convention.

September 8, 1787. The delegates appoint a Committee of Style to revise the rough draft of the Constitution.

September 12, 1787. The Committee of Style brings in the final version of the Constitution; Gouverneur Morris has done most of the rewriting.

September 17, 1787. All but three of the delegates present sign the Constitution; Benjamin Franklin discovers an omen for a happy future, and the Convention is adjourned.

September 28, 1787. Congress votes to send the Constitution to the states, to be ratified or rejected by popularly elected conventions.

October, 1787–1788. Alexander Hamilton, James Madison, and John Jay publish their *Federalist* essays in various New York newspapers; these essays analyze and defend the Constitution.

December 7, 1787. Delaware becomes the first state to ratify the Constitution.

June 21, 1788. New Hampshire becomes the ninth state to ratify the Constitution, thus establishing the new frame of government.

July 4, 1788. Philadelphia celebrates the ratification of the Constitution by a grand "Federal Procession."

December 15, 1791. The Bill of Rights, consisting of the first ten amendments, is ratified by the required number of states and becomes a part of the Constitution.

January 8, 1798. The Eleventh Amendment is ratified; this prohibits the citizen of another state, or of a foreign nation, from suing a given state in a federal court.

September 25, 1804. The Twelfth Amendment is ratified; this provides for the Presidential electors to vote for the President on one ballot and for the Vice President on a separate ballot—so that both will be members of the same political party.

December 18, 1865. The Thirteenth Amendment is ratified; this prohibits slavery.

July 21, 1868. The Fourteenth Amendment is ratified; this guarantees full civil rights to all citizens and declares that none can be deprived of "life, liberty, or property, without due process of law."

March 30, 1870. The Fifteenth Amendment is ratified; this declares that neither federal nor state government can deprive a citizen of the right to vote because of "race, color, or previous condition of servitude."

February 25, 1913. The Sixteenth Amendment is ratified; this gives Congress the right to levy income taxes.

May 31, 1913. The Seventeenth Amendment is ratified; this provides for the popular election of Senators, in place of election by state legislatures.

January 29, 1919. The Eighteenth Amendment is ratified; this prohibits "the manufacture, sale, or transportation of intoxicating liquors."

August 26, 1920. The Nineteenth Amendment is ratified; this gives women the right to vote.

February 6, 1933. The Twentieth Amendment is ratified; this changes the time for the inauguration of a new President from March to January 20 and also begins the term of the new Congress in January instead of March.

December 5, 1933. The Twenty-first Amendment is ratified; this repeals the Eighteenth Amendment, which had prohibited the manufacture and sale of alcoholic beverages.

February 26, 1951. The Twenty-second Amendment is ratified; this limits the President to two terms in office.

April 3, 1961. The Twenty-third Amendment is ratified; this permits residents of the District of Columbia to vote in Presidential elections.

January 23, 1964. The Twenty-fourth Amendment is ratified;

this prohibits the states from requiring that a poll tax be paid before a citizen can vote in Presidential or Congressional elections.

1971–1972. Congress approves an amendment guaranteeing equal rights for women, and submits it to the states for ratification; this declares "Equality of rights under the law shall not be denied or abridged by the United States or by any state on account of sex."

THE ARTICLES OF CONFEDERATION

To ALL to whom these Presents shall come, we the undersigned Delegates of the States affixed to our Names send greeting. Whereas the Delegates of the United States of America in Congress assembled did on the fifteenth day of November in the Year of our Lord One Thousand Seven Hundred and Seventy seven, and in the Second Year of the Independence of America agree to certain articles of Confederation and perpetual Union between the States of New-hampshire, Massachusetts-bay, Rhode-island and Providence Plantations, Connecticut, New York, New Jersey, Pennsylvania, Delaware, Maryland, Virginia, North-Carolina, South-Carolina and Georgia in the Words following, viz. "Articles of Confederation and perpetual Union between the states of Newhampshire, Massachusetts-bay, Rhode-island and Providence Plantations, Connecticut, New-York, New-Jersey, Pennsylvania, Delaware, Maryland, Virginia, North-Carolina, South-Carolina, and Georgia."

Art. I. The Stile of this confederacy shall be "The United States of America."

Art. II. Each state retains its sovereignty, freedom and independence, and every Power, Jurisdiction and right, which is not by this confederation expressly delegated to the United States, in Congress assembled.

Art. III. The said states hereby severally enter into a firm league of friendship with each other, for their common defence, the security of their Liberties, and their mutual and general welfare, binding themselves to assist each other, against all force offered to, or attacks made upon them, or any of them, on account of religion, sovereignty, trade, or any other pretence whatever.

Art. IV. The better to secure and perpetuate mutual friendship and intercourse among the people of the different states in this union, the free inhabitants of each of these states, paupers, vagabonds and fugitives from Justice excepted, shall be entitled to all privileges and immunities of free citizens in the several states; and the people of each state shall have free ingress and regress to and from any other state, and shall enjoy therein all the privileges of trade and commerce, subject to the same duties, impositions and restrictions as the inhabitants thereof respectively, provided that such restriction shall not extend so far as to prevent the removal of property imported into any state, to any other state of which the Owner is an inhabitant; provided also that no imposition, duties or restriction shall be laid by any state, on the property of the united states, or either of them.

If any Person guilty of, or charged with treason, felony, or other high misdemeanor in any state, shall flee from Justice, and be found in any of the united states, he shall upon demand of the Governor or executive power, of the state from which he fled, be delivered up and removed to the state having jurisdiction of his offence.

Full faith and credit shall be given in each of these states to the records, acts and judicial proceedings of the courts and magistrates of every other state.

Art. V. For the more convenient management of the general interests of the united states, delegates shall be annually appointed in such manner as the legislature of each state shall direct, to meet in Congress on the first Monday in November, in every year, with a power reserved to each state, to recall its delegates, or any of them, at any time within the year, and to send others in their stead, for the remainder of the Year.

No state shall be represented in Congress by less than two, nor by more than seven Members; and no person shall be capable of being a delegate for more than three years in any term of six years; nor shall any person, being a delegate, be capable of holding any office under the united states, for which he, or another for his benefit receives any salary, fees or emolument of any kind.

Each state shall maintain its own delegates in a meeting of the states, and while they act as members of the committee of the states.

In determining questions in the united states, in Congress assembled, each state shall have one vote.

Freedom of speech and debate in Congress shall not be impeached or questioned in any Court, or place out of Congress, and the members of congress shall be protected in their persons from arrests and imprisonments, during the time of their going to and from, and attendance on congress, except for treason, felony, or breach of the peace.

Art. VI. No state without the Consent of the united states in congress assembled, shall send any embassy to, or receive any embassy from, or enter into any conference, agreement, or alliance or treaty with any King, prince or state; nor shall any person holding any office of profit or trust under the united states, or any of them, accept of any present, emolument, office or title of any kind whatever from any king, prince or foreign state; nor shall the united states in congress assembled, or any of them, grant any title of nobility.

No two or more states shall enter into any treaty, confederation or alliance whatever between them, without the consent of the united states in congress assembled, specifying accurately the purposes for which the same is to be entered into, and how long it shall continue.

No state shall lay any imposts or duties, which may interfere with any stipulations in treaties, entered into by the united states in congress assembled, with any king, prince or state, in pursuance of any treaties already proposed by congress, to the courts of France and Spain.

No vessels of war shall be kept up in time of peace by any state, except such number only, as shall be deemed necessary by the united states in congress assembled, for the defence of such state, or its trade; nor shall any body of forces be kept up by any state, in time of peace, except such number only, as in the judgment of the united states, in congress assembled, shall be deemed requisite to garrison the forts necessary for the defence of such state; but every state shall always keep up a well regulated and disciplined militia, sufficiently armed and accoutred, and shall provide and constantly have ready for use, in public stores, a due number of field pieces and tents, and a proper quantity of arms, ammunition and camp equipage.

No state shall engage in any war without the consent of the united states in congress assembled, unless such state be actually invaded by enemies, or shall have received certain advice of a resolution being formed by some nation of Indians to invade such state, and the danger is so imminent as not to admit of a delay, till the united states in congress assembled can be consulted: nor shall any state grant commissions to any ships or vessels of war, nor letters of marque or reprisal, except it be after a declaration of war by the united states in congress assembled, and then only against the kingdom or state and the subjects thereof, against which war has been so declared, and under such regulations as shall be established by the united states in congress assembled, unless such state be infested by pirates, in which case vessels of war may be fitted out for that occasion, and kept so long as the danger shall continue, or until the united states in congress assembled shall determine otherwise.

Art. VII. When land-forces are raised by any state for the common defence, all officers of or under the rank of colonel, shall be appointed by the legislature of each state respectively by whom such forces shall be raised, or in such manner as such state shall direct, and all vacancies shall be filled up by the state which first made the appointment.

Art. VIII. All charges of war, and all other expences that shall be incurred for the common defence or general welfare, and allowed by the united states in congress assembled, shall be defrayed out of a common treasury, which shall be supplied by the several states, in proportion to the value of all land within each state, granted to or surveyed for any Person, as such land and the buildings and improvements thereon shall be estimated according to such mode as the united states in congress assembled, shall from time to time direct and appoint. The taxes for paying that proportion shall be laid and levied by the authority and direction of the legislatures of the several states within the time agreed upon by the united states in congress assembled.

Art. IX. The united states in congress assembled, shall have the sole and exclusive right and power of determining on peace and war, except in the cases mentioned in the sixth article—of sending and receiving ambassadors—entering into treaties and alliances, provided that no treaty of commerce shall be made whereby the legislative power of the respective states shall be restrained from imposing such imposts and duties on foreigners, as their own people are subjected to, or from prohibiting the exportation or importation of any species of goods or commodities whatsoever—of establishing rules for deciding in all cases, what captures on land or water shall be legal, and in what manner prizes taken by land or naval forces in the service of the united states shall be divided or appropriated—of granting letters of marque and reprisal in times of peace—appointing courts for the trial of piracies and felonies committed on the high seas and establishing courts for receiving and determining finally appeals in all cases of captures, provided that no member of congress shall be appointed a judge of any of the said courts.

The united states in congress assembled shall also be the last resort on appeal in all disputes and differences now subsisting or that hereafter may arise between two or more states concerning boundary, jurisdiction or any other cause whatever; which authority shall always be exercised in the manner following. Whenever the legislative or executive authority or lawful agent of any state in controversy with another shall present a petition to congress, stating the matter in question and praying for a hearing, notice thereof shall be given by order of congress to the legislative or executive authority of the other state in controversy, and a day assigned for the appearance of the parties by their lawful agents, who shall then be directed to appoint by joint consent, commissioners or judges to constitute a court for hearing and determining the matter in question: but if they cannot agree, congress shall name three persons out of each of the united states, and from the list of such persons each party shall alternately strike out one, the petitioners beginning, until the number shall be reduced to thirteen; and from that number not less then seven, nor more than nine names as congress shall direct, shall in the presence of congress be drawn out by lot, and the persons whose names shall be so drawn or any five of them, shall be commissioners or judges, to hear and finally determine the controversy, so always as a major part of the judges who shall hear the cause shall agree in the determination: and if either party shall neglect to attend at the day appointed, without shewing reasons, which congress shall judge sufficient, or being present shall refuse to strike, the congress shall proceed to nominate three persons out of each state, and the secretary of congress shall strike in behalf of such party absent or refusing; and the judgment and sentence of the court to be appointed, in the manner before prescribed, shall be final and conclusive; and if any of the parties shall refuse to submit to the authority of such court, or to appear to defend their claim, or cause, the court shall nevertheless proceed to pronounce sentence, or judgment, which shall in like manner be final and decisive, the judgment or sentence and other proceedings being in either case transmitted to congress, and lodged among the acts of congress for the security of the parties concerned: provided that every commissioner, before he sits in judgment, shall take an oath to be administered by one of the judges of the supreme or superior court of the state, where the cause shall be tried, "well and truly to hear and determine the matter in question, according to the best of his judgment, without favour, affection or hope of reward:" provided also that no state shall be deprived of territory for the benefit of the united states.

All controversies concerning the private right of soil claimed under different grants of two or more states, whose jurisdictions as they may respect such lands, and the states which passed such grants are adjusted, the said grants or either of them being at the same time claimed to have originated antecedent to such settlement of jursidiction, shall on the petition of either party to the congress of the united states, be finally determined as near as may be in the same manner as is before prescribed for deciding disputes respecting territorial jurisdiction between different states.

The united states in congress assembled shall also have the sole and exclusive right and power of regulating the alloy and value of coin struck by their own authority, or by that of the respective states—fixing the standard of weights and measures throughout the united states—regulating the trade and managing all affairs with the Indians, not members of any of the states, provided that the legislative right of any state within its own limits be not infringed or violated—establishing and regulating post-offices from one state to another, throughout all the united states, and exacting such postage on the papers passing thro' the same as may be requisite to defray the expences of the said office—appointing all officers of the land forces, in the service of the united states, excepting regimental officers—appointing all the officers of the naval forces, and commissioning all officers whatever in the service of the united states— making rules for the government and regulation of the said land and naval forces, and directing their operations.

The united states in congress assembled shall have authority to appoint a committee, to sit in the recess of congress, to be denominated "A Committee of the States," and to consist of one delegate from each state; and to appoint such other committees and civil officers as may be necessary for managing the general affairs of the united states under their direction—to appoint one of their number to preside, provided that no person be allowed to serve in the office of president more than one year in any term of three years; to ascertain the necessary sums of Money to be raised for the service of the united states, and to appropriate and apply the same for defraying the public expences—to borrow money, or emit bills on the credit of the united states, transmitting every half year to the respective states an account of the sums of money so borrowed or emitted—to build and equip a navy—to agree upon the number of land forces, and to make requisitions from each state for its quota, in proportion to the number of white inhabitants in such state: which requisition shall be binding, and thereupon the legislature of each state shall appoint the regimental officers, raise the men and cloath, arm and equip them in a soldier like manner, at the expence of the united states, and the officers and men so cloathed, armed and equipped shall march to the place appointed, and within the time agreed on by the united states in congress assembled: But if the united states in congress assembled shall, on consideration of circumstances judge proper that any state should not raise men, or should raise a smaller number than its quota, and that any other state should raise a greater number of men than the quota thereof, such extra number shall be raised, officered, cloathed, armed and equipped in the same manner as the quota of such state, unless the legislature of such state shall judge that such extra number cannot be safely spared out of the same, in which case they shall raise, officer, cloath, arm and equip as many of such extra number as they judge can be safely spared. And the officers and men so cloathed, armed and equipped, shall march to the place appointed, and within the time agreed on by the united states in congress assembled.

The united states in congress assembled shall never engage in a war, nor grant letters of marque and reprisal in time of peace, nor enter into any treaties or alliances, nor coin money, nor regulate the value thereof, nor ascertain the sums and expences necessary for the defence and welfare of the united states, or any of them, nor emit bills, nor borrow money on the credit of the united states, nor appropriate money, nor agree upon the number of vessels of war, to be built or purchased, or the number of land or sea forces to be raised, nor appoint a commander in chief of the army or navy, unless nine states assent to the same: nor shall a question on any other point, except for adjourning from day to day be determined, unless by the votes of a majority of the united states in congress assembled.

The congress of the united states shall have power to adjourn to any time within the year, and to any place within the united states, so that no period of adjournment be for a longer duration than the space of six Months, and shall publish the Journal of their proceedings monthly, except such parts thereof relating to treaties, alliances or military operations as in their judgment require secresy; and the yeas and nays of the delegates of each state on any question shall be entered on the Journal, when it is desired by any delegate; and the delegates of a state, or any of them, at his or their request shall be furnished with a transcript of the said Journal, except such parts as are above excepted, to lay before the legislatures of the several states.

Art. X. The committee of the states, or any nine of them, shall be authorised to execute, in the recess of congress, such of the powers of congress as the united states in congress assembled, by the consent of nine states, shall from time to time think expedient to vest them with; provided that no power be delegated to the said committee, for the exercise of which by the articles of confederation, the voice of nine states in the congress of the united states assembled is requisite.

Art. XI. Canada acceding to this confederation, and joining in the measures of the united states, shall be admitted into, and entitled to all the advantages of this union: but no other colony shall be admitted into the same, unless such admission be agreed to by nine states.

Art. XII. All bills of credit emitted, monies borrowed and debts contracted by, or under the authority of congress, before the assembling of the united states, in pursuance of the present confederation, shall be deemed and considered as a charge against the united states, for payment and satisfaction whereof the said united states, and the public faith are hereby solemnly pledged.

Art. XIII. Every state shall abide by the determinations of the united states in congress assembled, on all questions which by this confederation are submitted to them. And the Articles of this confederation shall be inviolably observed by every state, and the union shall be perpetual; nor shall any alteration at any time hereafter be made in any of them; unless such alteration be agreed to in a congress of the united states, and be afterwards confirmed by the legislatures of every state.

AND WHEREAS it hath pleased the Great Governor of the World to incline the hearts of the legislatures we respectively represent in congress, to approve of, and to authorize us to ratify the said articles of confederation and perpetual union. KNOW YE that we the undersigned delegates, by virtue of the power and authority to us given for that purpose, do by these presents, in the name and in behalf of our respective constituents, fully and entirely ratify and confirm each and every of the said articles of confederation and perpetual union, and all and singular the matters and things therein contained: And we do further solemnly plight and engage the faith of our respective constituents, that they shall abide by the determinations of the united states in congress assembled, on all questions, which by the said confederation are submitted to them. And that the articles thereof shall be inviolably observed by the states we respectively represent, and that the union shall be perpetual. In Witness thereof we have hereunto set our hands in Congress. Done at Philadelphia in the state of Pennsylvania the ninth Day of July in the Year of our Lord one Thousand seven Hundred and Seventy-eight, and in the third year of the independence of America.

JOSIAH BARTLETT
JOHN WENTWORTH Junr
   August 8th 1778

On the part and behalf of the
State of New Hampshire

JOHN HANCOCK
SAMUEL ADAMS
ELBRIDGE GERRY
FRANCIS DANA
JAMES LOVELL
SAMUEL HOLTEN

On the part and behalf of
The State of Massachusetts
Bay

185

WILLIAM ELLERY HENRY MARCHANT JOHN COLLINS	On the part and behalf of the State of Rhode-Island and Providence Plantations
ROGER SHERMAN SAMUEL HUNTINGTON OLIVER WOLCOTT TITUS HOSMER ANDREW ADAMS	On the part and behalf of the State of Connecticut
JA^S DUANE FRA^S LEWIS W^M DUER GOUV MORRIS	On the part and behalf of the State of New York
JNO WITHERSPOON NATH^L SCUDDER	On the part and behalf of the State of New Jersey. Novr 26, 1778.—
ROB^T MORRIS DANIEL ROBERDEAU JON^A BAYARD SMITH WILLIAM CLINGAN JOSEPH REED 22^d July 1778	On the part and behalf of the State of Pennsylvania
THO M:KEAN Feby 12 1779 JOHN DICKINSON May 5th 1779 NICHOLAS VAN DYKE	On the part and behalf of the State of Delaware
JOHN HANSON March 1 1781 DANIEL CARROLL d^o	On the part and behalf of the State of Maryland
RICHARD HENRY LEE JOHN BANISTER THOMAS ADAMS JN^O HARVIE FRANCIS LIGHTFOOT LEE	On the part and behalf of the State of Virginia

186

JOHN PENN July 21ˢᵗ 1778
CORNˢ HARNETT
JNᴼ WILLIAMS

> On the part and behalf of the
> State of Nᵒ Carolina

HENRY LAURENS
WILLIAM HENRY DRAYTON
JNᴼ MATHEWS
RICHᴰ HUTSON
THOˢ HEYWARD Junʳ

> On the part and behalf of the
> State of South-Carolina

JNᴼ WALTON 24ᵗʰ July
   1778
EDWᴰ TELFAIR
EDWᴰ LANGWORTHY

> On the part and behalf of the
> State of Georgia

THE CONSTITUTION OF THE UNITED STATES

WE THE PEOPLE of the United States, in Order to form a more perfect Union, establish Justice, insure domestic Tranquility, provide for the common defence, promote the general Welfare, and secure the Blessings of Liberty to ourselves and our Posterity, do ordain and establish this CONSTITUTION for the United States of America.

ARTICLE I

SECTION 1. All legislative Powers herein granted shall be vested in a Congress of the United States, which shall consist of a Senate and House of Representatives.

SECTION 2. The House of Representatives shall be composed of Members chosen every second Year by the People of the several States, and the Electors in each State shall have the Qualifications requisite for Electors of the most numerous Branch of the State Legislature.

No Person shall be a Representative who shall not have attained to the Age of twenty five Years, and been seven Years a Citizen of the United States, and who shall not, when elected, be an Inhabitant of that State in which he shall be chosen.

Representatives and direct Taxes shall be apportioned among the several States which may be included within this Union, according to their respective Numbers, which shall be determined by adding to the whole Number of free Persons, including those bound to Service for a Term of Years, and excluding Indians not taxed, three fifths of all other Persons. The actual Enumeration shall be made within three Years after the first Meeting of the Congress of the United States, and within every subsequent Term of ten Years, in such Manner as they shall by Law direct. The Number of Representatives shall not exceed one for every thirty Thousand, but each State shall have at Least one Representative; and until such enumeration shall be made, the State of New Hampshire shall be entitled to chuse three, Massachusetts eight, Rhode-Island and Providence Plantations one, Connecticut five, New-York six, New Jersey four, Pennsylvania eight, Delaware one, Maryland six, Virginia ten, North Carolina five, South Carolina five, and Georgia three.

When vacancies happen in the Representation from any State, the Executive Authority thereof shall issue Writs of Election to fill such Vacancies.

The House of Representatives shall chuse their Speaker and other Officers; and shall have the sole Power of Impeachment.

SECTION 3. The Senate of the United States shall be composed of two Senators from each State, chosen by the Legislature thereof, for six Years; and each Senator shall have one Vote.

Immediately after they shall be assembled in Consequence of the first Election, they shall be divided as equally as may be into three Classes. The Seats of the Senators of the first Class shall be vacated at the Expiration of the second Year, of the second Class at the Expiration of the fourth Year, and of the third Class at the Expiration of the sixth Year, so that one third may be chosen every second Year; and if Vacancies happen by Resignation, or otherwise, during the Recess of the Legislature of any State, the Executive thereof may make temporary Appointments until the next Meeting of the Legislature, which shall then fill such Vacancies.

No Person shall be a Senator who shall not have attained to the Age of thirty Years, and been nine Years a Citizen of the United States, and who shall not, when elected, be an Inhabitant of that State for which he shall be chosen.

The Vice President of the United States shall be President of the Senate, but shall have no Vote, unless they be equally divided.

The Senate shall chuse their other Officers, and also a President pro tempore, in the Absence of the Vice President, or when he shall exercise the Office of President of the United States.

The Senate shall have the sole Power to try all Impeachments. When sitting for that Purpose, they shall be on Oath or Affirmation. When the President of the United States is tried, the Chief

Justice shall preside: And no Person shall be convicted without the Concurrence of two thirds of the Members present.

Judgment in Cases of Impeachment shall not extend further than to removal from Office, and disqualification to hold and enjoy any Office of honor, Trust or Profit under the United States: but the Party convicted shall nevertheless be liable and subject to Indictment, Trial, Judgment and Punishment, according to Law.

SECTION 4. The Times, Places and Manner of holding Elections for Senators and Representatives, shall be prescribed in each State by the Legislature thereof; but the Congress may at any time by Law make or alter such Regulations, except as to the Places of chusing Senators.

The Congress shall assemble at least once in every Year, and such Meeting shall be on the first Monday in December, unless they shall by Law appoint a different Day.

SECTION 5. Each House shall be the Judge of the Elections, Returns and Qualifications of its own Members, and a Majority of each shall constitute a Quorum to do Business; but a smaller Number may adjourn from day to day, and may be authorized to compel the Attendance of absent Members, in such Manner, and under such Penalties as each House may provide.

Each House may determine the Rules of its Proceedings, punish its Members for disorderly Behaviour, and, with the Concurrence of two thirds, expel a Member.

Each House shall keep a Journal of its Proceedings, and from time to time publish the same, excepting such Parts as may in their Judgment require Secrecy; and the Yeas and Nays of the Members of either House on any question shall, at the desire of one fifth of those Present, be entered on the Journal.

Neither House, during the Session of Congress, shall, without the Consent of the other, adjourn for more than three days, nor to any other Place than that in which the two Houses shall be sitting.

SECTION 6. The Senators and Representatives shall receive a Compensation for their Services, to be ascertained by Law, and paid out of the Treasury of the United States. They shall in all Cases, except Treason, Felony and Breach of the Peace, be privileged from Arrest during their Attendance at the Session of their respective Houses, and in going to and returning from the same; and for any Speech or Debate in either House, they shall not be questioned in any other Place.

No Senator or Representative shall, during the Time for which he was elected, be appointed to any civil Office under the Authority of the United States, which shall have been created, or the Emoluments whereof shall have been encreased during such time; and no Person holding any Office under the United States, shall be a Member of either House during his Continuance in Office.

SECTION 7. All Bills for raising Revenue shall originate in the House of Representatives; but the Senate may propose or concur with Amendments as on other Bills.

Every Bill which shall have passed the House of Representatives and the Senate, shall, before it become a Law, be presented to the President of the United States; If he approve he shall sign it, but if not he shall return it, with his Objections to that House in which it shall have originated, who shall enter the Objections at large on their Journal, and proceed to reconsider it. If after such Reconsideration two thirds of that House shall agree to pass the Bill, it shall be sent, together with the Objections, to the other House, by which it shall likewise be reconsidered, and if approved by two thirds of that House, it shall become a Law. But in all such Cases the Votes of both Houses shall be determined by yeas and Nays, and the Names of the Persons voting for and against the Bill shall be entered on the Journal of each House respectively. If any Bill shall not be returned by the President within ten Days (Sundays excepted) after it shall have been presented to him, the Same shall be a Law, in like Manner as if he had signed it, unless the Congress by their Adjournment prevent its Return, in which Case it shall not be a Law.

Every Order, Resolution, or Vote to which the Concurrence of the Senate and House of Representatives may be necessary (except on a question of Adjournment) shall be presented to the President of the United States; and before the Same shall take Effect, shall be approved by him, or being disapproved by him, shall be repassed by two thirds of the Senate and House of Representatives, according to the Rules and Limitations prescribed in the Case of a Bill.

SECTION 8. The Congress shall have Power to lay and collect Taxes, Duties, Imports and Excises, to pay the Debts and provide for the common Defence and general Welfare of the United States; but all Duties, Imposts and Excises shall be uniform throughout the United States;

To borrow Money on the credit of the United States;

To regulate Commerce with foreign Nations, and among the several States, and with the Indian Tribes;

To establish an uniform Rule of Naturalization, and uniform Laws on the subject of Bankruptcies throughout the United States;

To coin Money, regulate the Value thereof, and of foreign Coin, and fix the Standard of Weights and Measures;

To provide for the Punishment of counterfeiting the Securities and current Coin of the United States;

To establish Post Offices and post Roads;

To promote the Progress of Science and useful Arts, by securing for limited Times to Authors and Inventors the exclusive Right to their respective Writings and Discoveries;

To constitute Tribunals inferior to the supreme Court;

To define and punish Piracies and Felonies committed on the high Seas, and Offences against the Law of Nations;

To declare War, grant Letters of Marque and Reprisal, and make Rules concerning Captures on Land and Water;

To raise and support Armies, but no Appropriation of Money to that Use shall be for a longer Term than two Years;

To provide and maintain a Navy;

To make Rules for the Government and Regulation of the land and naval Forces;

To provide for calling forth the Militia to execute the Laws of the Union, suppress Insurrections and repel Invasions;

To provide for organizing, arming, and disciplining, the Militia, and for governing such Part of them as may be employed in the Service of the United States, reserving to the States respectively, the Appointment of the Officers, and the Authority of training the Militia according to the discipline prescribed by Congress;

To exercise exclusive Legislation in all Cases whatsoever, over such District (not exceeding ten Miles square) as may, by Cession of particular States, and the Acceptance of Congress, become the Seat of the Government of the United States, and to exercise like Authority over all Places purchased by the Consent of the Legislature of the State in which the Same shall be, for the Erection of

Forts, Magazines, Arsenals, dock-Yards, and other needful Buildings;—And

To make all Laws which shall be necessary and proper for carrying into Execution the foregoing Powers, and all other Powers vested by this Constitution in the Government of the United States, or in any Department or Officer thereof.

SECTION 9. The Migration or Importation of such Persons as any of the States now existing shall think proper to admit, shall not be prohibited by the Congress prior to the Year one thousand eight hundred and eight, but a Tax or duty may be imposed on such Importation, not exceeding ten dollars for each Person.

The Privilege of the Writ of Habeas Corpus shall not be suspended, unless when in Cases of Rebellion or Invasion the public Safety may require it.

No Bill of Attainder or ex post facto Law shall be passed.

No Capitation, or other direct, Tax shall be laid, unless in Proportion to the Census or Enumeration herein before directed to be taken.

No Tax or Duty shall be laid on Articles exported from any State.

No Preference shall be given by any Regulation of Commerce or Revenue to the Ports of one State over those of another: nor shall Vessels bound to, or from, one State, be obliged to enter, clear, or pay Duties in another.

No Money shall be drawn from the Treasury, but in Consequence of Appropriations made by Law; and a regular Statement and Account of the Receipts and Expenditures of all public Money shall be published from time to time.

No Title of Nobility shall be granted by the United States: And no Person holding any Office or Profit or Trust under them, shall, without the Consent of the Congress, accept of any present, Emolument, Office, or Title, of any kind whatever, from any King, Prince, or foreign State.

SECTION 10. No State shall enter into any Treaty, Alliance, or Confederation; grant Letters of Marque and Reprisal; coin Money; emit Bills of Credit; make any Thing but gold and silver Coin a Tender in Payment of Debts; pass any Bill of Attainder, ex post facto Law, or Law impairing the Obligation of Contracts, or grant any Title of Nobility.

No State shall, without the Consent of the Congress, lay any Imposts or Duties on Imports or Exports, except what may be absolutely necessary for executing its inspection Laws: and the net Produce of all Duties and Imposts, laid by any State on Imports or Exports, shall be for the Use of the Treasury of the United States; and all such Laws shall be subject to the Revision and Control of the Congress.

No State shall, without the Consent of Congress, lay any Duty of Tonnage, keep Troops, or Ships of War in time of Peace, enter into any Agreement or Compact with another State, or with a foreign Power, or engage in War, unless actually invaded, or in such imminent Danger as will not admit of delay.

ARTICLE II

SECTION 1. The executive Power shall be vested in a President of the United States of America. He shall hold his Office during the Term of four Years, and, together with the Vice President, chosen for the same Term, be elected, as follows

Each State shall appoint, in such Manner as the Legislature thereof may direct, a Number of Electors, equal to the whole Number of Senators and Representatives to which the State may be entitled in the Congress: but no Senator or Representative, or Person holding an Office of Trust or Profit under the United States, shall be appointed an Elector.

The Electors shall meet in their respective States, and vote by Ballot for two Persons, of whom one at least shall not be an Inhabitant of the same State with themselves. And they shall make a List of all the Persons voted for, and of the Number of Votes for each; which List they shall sign and certify, and transmit sealed to the Seat of the Government of the United States, directed to the President of the Senate. The President of the Senate shall, in the Presence of the Senate and House of Representatives, open all the Certificates, and the Votes shall then be counted. The Person having the greatest Number of Votes shall be the President, if such Number be a Majority of the whole Number of Electors appointed; and if there be more than one who have such Majority, and have an equal Number of Votes, then the House of Representatives shall immediately chuse by Ballot one of them for President; and if no

Person have a Majority, then from the five highest on the List the said House shall in like Manner chuse the President. But in chusing the President, the Votes shall be taken by States, the Representation from each State having one Vote; A quorum for this Purpose shall consist of a Member or Members from two thirds of the States, and a Majority of all the States shall be necessary to a Choice. In every Case, after the Choice of the President, the Person having the greatest Number of Votes of the Electors shall be the Vice President. But if there should remain two or more who have equal Votes, the Senate shall chuse from them by Ballot the Vice President.

The Congress may determine the Time of chusing the Electors, and the Day on which they shall give their Votes; which Day shall be the same throughout the United States.

No Person except a natural born Citizen, or a Citizen of the United States, at the time of the Adoption of this Constitution, shall be eligible to the Office of President; neither shall any Person be eligible to that Office who shall not have attained to the Age of thirty five Years, and been fourteen Years a Resident within the United States.

In Case of the Removal of the President from Office, or of his Death, Resignation, or Inability to discharge the Powers and Duties of the said Office, the Same shall devolve on the Vice President, and the Congress may by Law provide for the Case of Removal, Death, Resignation or Inability, both of the President and Vice President, declaring what Officer shall then act as President, and such Officer shall act accordingly, until the Disability be removed, or a President shall be elected.

The President shall, at stated Times, receive for his Services, a Compensation, which shall neither be encreased nor diminished during the Period for which he shall have been elected, and he shall not receive within that Period any other Emolument from the United States, or any of them.

Before he enter on the Execution of his Office, he shall take the following Oath or Affirmation:—"I do solemnly swear (or affirm) that I will faithfully execute the Office of President of the United States, and will to the best of my Ability, preserve, protect and defend the Constitution of the United States."

SECTION 2. The President shall be Commander in Chief of the

Army and Navy of the United States, and of the Militia of the several States, when called into the actual Service of the United States; he may require the Opinion, in writing, of the principal Officer in each of the executive Departments, upon any Subject relating to the Duties of their respective Offices, and he shall have Power to grant Reprieves and Pardons for Offences against the United States, except in Cases of Impeachment.

He shall have Power, by and with the Advice and Consent of the Senate, to make Treaties, provided two thirds of the Senators present concur; and he shall nominate, and by and with the Advice and Consent of the Senate, shall appoint Ambassadors, other public Ministers and Consuls, Judges of the supreme Court, and all other Officers of the United States, whose Appointments are not herein otherwise provided for, and which shall be established by Law: but the Congress may by Law vest the Appointment of such inferior Officers, as they think proper, in the President alone, in the Courts of Law, or in the Heads of Departments.

The President shall have Power to fill up all Vacancies that may happen during the Recess of the Senate, by granting Commissions which shall expire at the End of their next Session.

SECTION 3. He shall from time to time give to the Congress Information of the State of the Union, and recommend to their Consideration such Measures as he shall judge necessary and expedient; he may, on extraordinary Occasions, convene both Houses, or either of them, and in Case of Disagreement between them, with Respect to the Time of Adjournment, he may adjourn them to such Time as he shall think proper; he shall receive Ambassadors and other public Ministers; he shall take Care that the Laws be faithfully executed, and shall Commission all the Officers of the United States.

SECTION 4. The President, Vice President and all civil Officers of the United States, shall be removed from Office on Impeachment for, and Conviction of, Treason, Bribery, or other high Crimes and Misdemeanors.

ARTICLE III

SECTION 1. The judicial Power of the United States, shall be vested in one supreme Court, and in such inferior Courts as the Congress may from time to time ordain and establish. The Judges, both of the supreme and inferior Courts, shall hold their Offices during good Behaviour, and shall, at stated Times, receive for their Services, a Compensation, which shall not be diminished during their continuance in Office.

SECTION 2. The judicial Power shall extend to all Cases, in Law and Equity, arising under this Constitution, the Laws of the United States, and Treaties made, or which shall be made, under their Authority;—to all Cases affecting Ambassadors, other public Ministers and Consuls;—to all Cases of admiralty and maritime Jurisdiction;—to Controversies to which the United States shall be a Party;—to Controversies between two or more States;—between a State and Citizens of another State;—between Citizens of different States,—between Citizens of the same State claiming Lands under Grants of different States, and between a State, or the Citizens thereof, and foreign States, Citizens or Subjects.

In all Cases affecting Ambassadors, other public Ministers and Consuls, and those in which a State shall be Party, the supreme Court shall have original Jurisdiction. In all the other Cases before mentioned, the supreme Court shall have appellate Jurisdiction, both as to Law and Fact, with such Exceptions, and under such regulations as the Congress shall make.

The Trial of all Crimes, except in Cases of Impeachment, shall be by Jury; and such Trial shall be held in the State where the said Crimes shall have been committed; but when not committed within any State, the Trial shall be at such Place or Places as the Congress may by Law have directed.

SECTION 3. Treason against the United States, shall consist only in levying War against them, or in adhering to their Enemies, giving them Aid and Comfort. No person shall be convicted of Treason unless on the Testimony of two Witnesses to the same overt Act, or on Confession in open Court.

The Congress shall have Power to declare the Punishment of Treason, but no Attainder of Treason shall work Corruption of Blood, or Forfeiture except during the Life of the Person attainted.

ARTICLE IV

SECTION 1. Full Faith and Credit shall be given in each State to the public Acts, Records, and judicial Proceedings of every other State.

And the Congress may by general Laws prescribe the Manner in which such Acts, Records and Proceedings shall be proved, and the Effect thereof.

SECTION 2. The Citizens of each State shall be entitled to all Privileges and Immunities of Citizens in the several States.

A Person charged in any State with Treason, Felony, or other Crime, who shall flee from Justice, and be found in another State, shall on demand of the executive Authority of the State from which he fled, be delivered up, to be removed to the State having Jurisdiction of the Crime.

No Person held to Service or Labour in one State, under the Laws thereof, escaping into another, shall, in Consequence of any Law or Regulation therein, be discharged from such Service or Labour, but shall be delivered up on Claim of the Party to whom such Service or Labour may be due.

SECTION 3. New States may be admitted by the Congress into this Union; but no new State shall be formed or erected within the Jurisdiction of any other State; nor any State be formed by the Junction of two or more States, or Parts of States, without the Consent of the Legislatures of the States concerned as well as of the Congress.

The Congress shall have Power to dispose of and make all needful Rules and Regulations respecting the Territory or other Property belonging to the United States; and nothing in this Constitution shall be so construed as to Prejudice any Claims of the United States, or of any particular State.

SECTION 4. The United States shall guarantee to every State in this Union a Republican Form of Government, and shall protect each of them against Invasion; and on Application of the Legislature, or of the Executive (when the Legislature cannot be convened) against domestic Violence.

ARTICLE V

The Congress, whenever two thirds of both Houses shall deem it necessary, shall propose Amendments to this Constitution, or, on the Application of the Legislatures of two thirds of the several States, shall call a convention for proposing Amendments, which, in either Case, shall be valid to all Intents and Purposes, as Part of this Constitution, when ratified by the Legislatures of three fourths of the several States, or by Conventions in three fourths thereof, as the one or the other Mode of Ratification may be proposed by the Congress; Provided that no Amendment which may be made prior to the Year One thousand eight hundred and eight shall in any Manner affect the first and fourth Clauses in the Ninth Section of the first Article; and that no State, without its Consent, shall be deprived of its equal Suffrage in the Senate.

ARTICLE VI

All Debts contracted and Engagements entered into, before the Adoption of this Constitution, shall be valid against the United States under this Constitution, as under the Confederation.

This Constitution, and the Laws of the United States which shall be made in Pursuance thereof; and all Treaties made, or which shall be made, under the Authority of the United States, shall be the supreme Law of the Land; and the Judges in every State shall be bound thereby, any Thing in the Constitution or Laws of any State to the Contrary notwithstanding.

The Senators and Representatives before mentioned, and the Members of the several State Legislatures, and all executive and judicial Officers, both of the United States and of the several States, shall be bound by Oath or Affirmation, to support this Constitution; but no religious Test shall ever be required as a Qualification to any Office or public Trust under the United States.

ARTICLE VII

The Ratification of the Conventions of nine States, shall be sufficient for the Establishment of this Constitution between the States so ratifying the Same.

Done in Convention by the Unanimous Consent of the States present the Seventeenth Day of September in the Year of our Lord one thousand seven hundred and eighty seven and of the Independence of the United States of America the Twelfth In Witness whereof We have hereunto subscribed our Names,

George Washington—President and deputy from Virginia
Attest WILLIAM JACKSON *Secretary*

New Hampshire	{ JOHN LANGDON NICHOLAS GILMAN
Massachusetts	{ NATHANIEL GORHAM RUFUS KING
Connecticut	{ WM: SAML. JOHNSON ROGER SHERMAN
New York	ALEXANDER HAMILTON
New Jersey	{ WIL: LIVINGSTON DAVID BREARLEY WM. PATERSON JONA: DAYTON
Pennsylvania	{ B. FRANKLIN THOMAS MIFFLIN ROBT. MORRIS GEO. CLYMER THOS. FITZ SIMONS JARED INGERSOLL JAMES WILSON GOUV MORRIS
Delaware	{ GEO: READ GUNNING BEDFORD jun JOHN DICKINSON RICHARD BASSETT JACO: BROOM
Maryland	{ JAMES MCHENRY DAN OF ST THOS. JENIFER DANL CARROLL
Virginia	{ JOHN BLAIR JAMES MADISON JR.
North Carolina	{ WM: BLOUNT RICHD. DOBBS SPAIGHT HU WILLIAMSON

South Carolina
$\left\{\begin{array}{l}\text{J. RUTLEDGE} \\ \text{CHARLES COTESWORTH PINCKNEY} \\ \text{CHARLES PINCKNEY} \\ \text{PIERCE BUTLER}\end{array}\right.$

Georgia
$\left\{\begin{array}{l}\text{WILLIAM FEW} \\ \text{ABR BALDWIN}\end{array}\right.$

AMENDMENTS

THE BILL OF RIGHTS

[December 15, 1791]

ARTICLE I

Congress shall make no law respecting an establishment of religion, or prohibiting the free exercise thereof; or abridging the freedom of speech, or of the press; or the right of the people peaceably to assemble, and to petition the Government for a redress of grievances.

ARTICLE II

A well regulated Militia, being necessary to the security of a free State, the right of the people to keep and bear Arms, shall not be infringed.

ARTICLE III

No Soldier shall, in time of peace be quartered in any house, without the consent of the Owner, nor in time of war, but in a manner to be prescribed by law.

ARTICLE IV

The right of the people to be secure in their persons, houses, papers, and effects, against unreasonable searches and seizures, shall not be violated, and no Warrants shall issue, but upon probable cause, supported by Oath or affirmation, and particularly describing the place to be searched, and the persons or things to be seized.

No person shall be held to answer for a capital, or otherwise infamous crime, unless on a presentment or indictment of a Grand Jury, except in cases arising in the land or naval forces, or in the Militia, when in actual service in time of War or public danger; nor shall any person be subject for the same offence to be twice put in jeopardy of life or limb; nor shall be compelled in any Criminal Case to be a witness against himself, nor be deprived of life, liberty, or property, without due process of law; nor shall private property be taken for public use, without just compensation.

In all criminal prosecutions, the accused shall enjoy the right to a speedy and public trial, by an impartial jury of the State and district wherein the crime shall have been committed, which district shall have been previously ascertained by law, and to be informed of the nature and cause of the accusation; to be confronted with the witnesses against him; to have compulsory process for obtaining witnesses in his favor, and to have the Assistance of Counsel for his defence.

In Suits at common law, where the value in controversy shall exceed twenty dollars, the right of trial by jury shall be preserved, and no fact tried by a jury, shall be otherwise re-examined in any Court of the United States, than according to the rules of the common law.

ARTICLE VIII

Excessive bail shall not be required, nor excessive fines imposed, nor cruel and unusual punishments inflicted.

ARTICLE IX

The enumeration in the Constitution, of certain rights, shall not be construed to deny or disparage others retained by the people.

ARTICLE X

The powers not delegated to the United States by the Constitution, nor prohibited by it to the States, are reserved to the States respectively, or to the people.

AMENDMENTS XI-XXIV

ARTICLE XI

[January 8, 1798]

The Judicial power of the United States shall not be construed to extend to any suit in law or equity, commenced or prosecuted against one of the United States by Citizens of another State, or by Citizens or Subjects of any Foreign State.

ARTICLE XII

[September 25, 1804]

The Electors shall meet in their respective states, and vote by ballot for President and Vice President, one of whom, at least, shall not be an inhabitant of the same state with themselves; they shall name in their ballots the person voted for as President, and in distinct ballots the person voted for as Vice-President, and they

204

shall make distinct lists of all persons voted for as President, and of all persons voted for as Vice-President, and of the number of votes for each, which lists they shall sign and certify, and transmit sealed to the seat of the government of the United States, directed to the President of the Senate;—The President of the Senate shall, in presence of the Senate and House of Representatives, open all the certificates and the votes shall then be counted;—The person having the greatest number of votes for President, shall be the President, if such number be a majority of the whole number of Electors appointed; and if no person have such majority, then from the persons having the highest numbers not exceeding three on the list of those voted for as President, the House of Representatives shall choose immediately, by ballot, the President. But in choosing the President, the votes shall be taken by states, the representation from each state having one vote; a quorum for this purpose shall consist of a member or members from two-thirds of the states, and a majority of all the states shall be necessary to a choice. And if the House of Representatives shall not choose a President whenever the right of choice shall devolve upon them, before the fourth day of March next following, then the Vice-President shall act as President, as in the case of the death or other constitutional disability of the President. The person having the greatest number of votes as Vice-President, shall be the Vice-President, if such number be a majority of the whole number of Electors appointed, and if no person have a majority, then from the two highest numbers on the list, the Senate shall choose the Vice-President; a quorum for the purpose shall consist of two-thirds of the whole number of Senators, and a majority of the whole number shall be necessary to a choice. But no person constitutionally ineligible to the office of President shall be eligible to that of Vice-President of the United States.

ARTICLE XIII

[December 18, 1865]

SECTION 1. Neither slavery nor involuntary servitude, except as a punishment for crime whereof the party shall have been duly convicted, shall exist within the United States, or any place subject to their jurisdiction.

SECTION 2. Congress shall have power to enforce this article by appropriate legislation.

[July 21, 1868]

SECTION 1. All persons born or naturalized in the United States, and subject to the jurisdiction thereof, are citizens of the United States and of the State wherein they reside. No State shall make or enforce any law which shall abridge the privileges or immunities of citizens of the United States; nor shall any State deprive any person of life, liberty, or property, without due process of law; nor deny to any person within its jurisdiction the equal protection of the laws.

SECTION 2. Representatives shall be apportioned among the several States according to their respective numbers, counting the whole number of persons in each State, excluding Indians not taxed. But when the right to vote at any election for the choice of electors for President and Vice President of the United States, Representatives in Congress, the Executive and Judicial officers of a State, or the members of the Legislature thereof, is denied to any of the male inhabitants of such State, being twenty-one years of age, and citizens of the United States, or in any way abridged, except for participation in rebellion, or other crime, the basis of representation therein shall be reduced in the proportion which the number of such male citizens shall bear to the whole number of male citizens twenty-one years of age in such State.

SECTION 3. No person shall be a Senator or Representative in Congress, or elector of President and Vice President, or hold any office, civil or military, under the United States, or under any State, who, having previously taken an oath, as a member of Congress, or as an officer of the United States, or as a member of any State legislature, or as an executive or judicial officer of any State, to support the Constitution of the United States, shall have engaged in insurrection or rebellion against the same, or given aid or comfort to the enemies thereof. But Congress may by a vote of two-thirds of each House, remove such disability.

SECTION 4. The validity of the public debt of the United States, authorized by law, including debts incurred for payment of pensions and bounties for services in suppressing insurrection or rebellion, shall not be questioned. But neither the United States nor any State shall assume or pay any debt or obligation incurred in aid of insurrection or rebellion against the United States, or any claim for the loss or emancipation of any slave; but all such debts, obligations and claims shall be held illegal and void.

SECTION 5. The Congress shall have power to enforce, by appropriate legislation, the provisions of this article.

ARTICLE XV

[March 30, 1870]

SECTION 1. The right of citizens of the United States to vote shall not be denied or abridged by the United States or by any State on account of race, color, or previous condition of servitude.

SECTION 2. The Congress shall have power to enforce this article by appropriate legislation.

ARTICLE XVI

[February 25, 1913]

The Congress shall have the power to lay and collect taxes on incomes, from whatever source derived, without apportionment among the several States, and without regard to any census or enumeration.

ARTICLE XVII

[May 31, 1913]

SECTION 1. The Senate of the United States shall be composed of two Senators from each State, elected by the people thereof, for six

207

years; and each Senator shall have one vote. The electors in each State shall have the qualifications requisite for electors of the most numerous branch of the State Legislatures.

SECTION 2. When vacancies happen in the representation of any State in the Senate, the executive authority of such State shall issue writs of election to fill such vacancies; Provided, That the Legislature of any State may empower the executive thereof to make temporary appointment until the people fill the vacancies by election as the Legislature may direct.

SECTION 3. This amendment shall not be so construed as to affect the election or term of any Senator chosen before it becomes valid as part of the Constitution.

ARTICLE XVIII

[January 29, 1919]

SECTION 1. After one year from the ratification of this article, the manufacture, sale, or transportation of intoxicating liquors within, the importation thereof into, or the exportation thereof from the United States and all territory subject to the jurisdiction thereof, for beverage purposes, is hereby prohibited.

SECTION 2. The Congress and the several States shall have concurrent power to enforce this article by appropriate legislation.

SECTION 3. This article shall be inoperative unless it shall have been ratified as an amendment to the Constitution by the legislatures of the several States, as provided in the Constitution, within seven years from the date of the submission hereof to the States by the Congress.

ARTICLE XIX

[August 26, 1920]

SECTION 1. The rights of citizens of the United States to vote, shall not be denied or abridged by the United States or by any State on account of sex.

208

Section 2. Congress shall have power to enforce this article by appropriate legislation.

[February 6, 1933]

Section 1. The terms of the President and Vice President shall end at noon on the twentieth day of January, and the terms of Senators and Representatives at noon on the third day of January, of the years in which such terms would have ended if this article had not been ratified; and the terms of their successors shall then begin.

Section 2. The Congress shall assemble at least once in every year, and such meeting shall begin at noon on the third day of January, unless they shall by law appoint a different day.

Section 3. If, as the time fixed for the beginning of the term of the President, the President elect shall have died, the Vice President elect shall become President. If a President shall not have been chosen before the time fixed for the beginning of his term, or if the President elect shall have failed to qualify, then the Vice President elect shall act as President until a President shall have qualified; and the Congress may by law provide for the case wherein neither a President elect nor a Vice President elect shall have qualified, declaring who shall then act as President, or the manner in which one who is to act shall be selected, and such person shall act accordingly until a President or Vice President shall have qualified.

Section 4. The Congress may by law provide for the case of the death of any of the persons from whom the House of Representatives may choose a President whenever the right of choice shall have devolved upon them, and for the case of the death of any of the persons from whom the Senate may choose a Vice President whenever the right of choice shall have devolved upon them.

Section 5. Sections 1 and 2 shall take effect on the fifteenth day of October following the ratification of this article.

Section 6. This article shall be inoperative unless it shall have been ratified as an amendment to the Constitution by the legislatures of three-fourths of the several States within seven years from the date of its submission.

ARTICLE XXI

[December 5, 1933]

SECTION 1. The eighteenth article of amendment to the Constitution of the United States is hereby repealed.

SECTION 2. The transportation or importation into any State, Territory, or possession of the United States for delivery or use therein of intoxicating liquors, in violation of the laws thereof, is hereby prohibited.

SECTION 3. This article shall be inoperative unless it shall have been ratified as an amendment to the Constitution by conventions in the several States, as provided in the Constitution, within seven years from the date of the submission hereof to the States by the Congress.

ARTICLE XXII

[February 26, 1951]

SECTION 1. No person shall be elected to the office of the President more than twice, and no person who has held the office of President, or acted as President for more than two years of a term to which some other person was elected President shall be elected to the office of the President more than once. But this Article shall not apply to any person holding the office of President when this Article was proposed by the Congress, and shall not prevent any person who may be holding the office of President, or acting as President, during the term within which this Article becomes operative from holding the office of President or acting as President during the remainder of such terms.

210

SECTION 2. This Article shall be inoperative unless it shall be ratified as an amendment to the Constitution by the Legislatures of three-fourths of the several States within seven years from the date of its submission to the States by the Congress.

ARTICLE XXIII

[April 3, 1961]

SECTION 1. The District constituting the seat of Government of the United States shall appoint in such number as the Congress may direct:

A number of electors of President and Vice President equal to the whole number of Senators and Representatives in Congress to which the District would be entitled if it were a State, but in no event more than the least populous State; they shall be in addition to those appointed by the States but they shall be considered, for the purposes of election of President and Vice President, to be electors appointed by a State; and they shall meet in the District and perform such duties as provided by the twelfth article of amendment.

SECTION 2. The Congress shall have power to enforce this article by appropriate legislation.

ARTICLE XXIV

[January 23, 1964]

SECTION 1. The right of citizens of the United States to vote in any primary or other election for President or Vice President, or for Senator or Representative in Congress, shall not be denied or abridged by the United States or any State by reason of failure to pay any poll tax or other tax.

[February 10, 1967]

SECTION 1. In case of the removal of the President from office or of his death or resignation, the Vice President shall become President.

SECTION 2. Whenever there is a vacancy in the office of the Vice President, the President shall nominate a Vice President who shall take office upon confirmation by a majority vote of both houses of Congress.

SECTION 3. Whenever the President transmits to the President pro tempore of the Senate and the Speaker of the House of Representatives his written declaration that he is unable to discharge the powers and duties of his office, and until he transmits to them a written declaration to the contrary, such powers and duties shall be discharged by the Vice President as Acting President.

SECTION 4. Whenever the Vice President and a majority of either the principal officers of the executive departments or of such other body as Congress may by law provide, transmit to the President pro tempore of the Senate and the Speaker of the House of Representatives their written declaration that the President is unable to discharge the powers and duties of his office, the Vice President shall immediately assume the powers and duties of the office as Acting President.

Thereafter, when the President transmits to the President pro tempore of the Senate and the Speaker of the House of Representatives his written declaration that no inability exists, he shall resume the powers and duties of his office unless the Vice President and a majority of either the principal officers of the executive department or of such other body as Congress may by law provide, transmit within four days to the President pro tempore of the Senate and the Speaker of the House of Representatives their written declaration that the President is unable to discharge the powers and duties of his office. Thereupon Congress shall decide the issue, assembling within forty-eight hours for that purpose if not in session. If the Congress, within twenty-one days after receipt of the latter written declaration, or, if Congress is not in session, within twenty-one days after Congress is required to assemble, determines by two-thirds vote of both houses that the President is unable to discharge the powers and duties of his office, the Vice President shall continue to discharge the same as Acting President; otherwise, the President shall resume the powers and duties of his office.

ARTICLE XXVI

[June 30, 1971]

SECTION 1. The right of citizens of the United States, who are 18 years of age or older, to vote shall not be denied or abridged by the United States or any state on account of age.

SECTION 2. The Congress shall have the power to enforce this article by appropriate legislation.

SELECTED BIBLIOGRAPHY

BOWEN, CATHERINE DRINKER, *Miracle at Philadelphia*. Boston, Little, Brown and Company, 1966. The most readable account of the Constitutional Convention—lively sketches of the delegates.

DOS PASSOS, JOHN, *The Men Who Made the Nation*. New York, Doubleday & Company, Inc., 1957. Early history, from Yorktown to the Hamilton-Burr duel, narrated with the suspense of a novel.

ELLIOT, JONATHAN, ed., *The Debates in the Several State Conventions*. Philadelphia, J. B. Lippincott & Co., 1881. 5 vols. Speeches for and against the Constitution in the state ratifying conventions.

FARRAND, MAX, *The Framing of the Constitution*. New Haven, Yale University Press, 1913. Concise, clear account of the writing of the Constitution, with appendix of key documents.

FARRAND, MAX, ed., *The Records of the Federal Convention of 1787*. New Haven, Yale University Press, 1937. 4 vols. Authoritative collection of the documents of the Constitutional Convention, including Madison's record, the official minutes, letters, diary entries, preliminary plans, etc.

HAMILTON, ALEXANDER; JAY, JOHN; and MADISON, JAMES, *The Federalist*, ed., E. M. Earle. New York, Random House, 1937. The most famous contemporary interpretation of the Constitution—classic defense of the American system of government.

JENSEN, MERRILL, *The New Nation*. New York, Alfred A. Knopf, 1950. The United States under the Articles of Confederation; a provocative defense of the Confederation period.

214

LEWIS, JOHN DONALD, *Anti-Federalists Versus Federalists.* San Francisco, Chandler Publishing Co., 1967. Well-chosen contemporary essays and speeches for and against the Constitution, with an introduction describing the struggle for ratification.

MCDONALD, FORREST, and MCDONALD, ELLEN SHAPIRO, *Confederation and Constitution, 1781–1789.* Columbia, S.C., University of South Carolina Press, 1968. Documents for the 1781–1789 period, with an introduction and headnotes which explain the historical background.

MITCHELL, BROADUS, and MITCHELL, LOUISE PEARSON, *A Biography of the Constitution of the United States.* New York, Oxford University Press, 1964. How the Constitution came to be written and how it has been interpreted since its adoption—scholarly, readable.

MORISON, SAMUEL ELIOT, *The Oxford History of the American People.* New York, Oxford University Press, 1965. The best general history of the American people—lively and enlightening for every period.

ROSSITER, CLINTON, *1787: The Grand Convention.* New York, The Macmillan Company, 1966. The most thorough and well-organized description of the Constitutional Convention, its actors, conflict of ideas, and accomplishment.

RUSSELL, FRANCIS, *Making of the Nation.* New York, American Heritage Publishing Co., Inc., 1968. A popular history, with many fascinating contemporary illustrations.

PHOTO CREDITS

Frontispiece. The Historical Society of Pennsylvania: "A N.W. View of the State House in Philadelphia."

Page 9. Historical Society of Delaware: Gunning Bedford.
Independence National Historical Park Collection: John Dickinson, by C. W. Peale; Benjamin Franklin, by Joseph S. Duplessis; Elbridge Gerry, by J. Bogle; Nathaniel Gorham, by A. Rosenthal.

Page 11. Baltimore Bar Library: Luther Martin.
Bowdoin College Museum of Art: James Madison, by Gilbert Stuart.
Independence National Historical Park Collection: William S. Johnson, attributed to Sharples; Rufus King, by C. W. Peale.

Page 13. Independence National Historical Park Collection: George Mason, by Thomas B. Welch; Gouverneur Morris, by E. D. Marchant; Robert Morris, by C. W. Peale; Charles Cotesworth Pinckney, by Sharples.
National Museum, Philadelphia: William Paterson, by A. Rosenthal.

Page 15. Independence National Historical Park Collection: John Rutledge, by A. Rosenthal; Roger Sherman, by Thomas Hicks; Hugh Williamson, by A. Rosenthal; James Wilson, by A. Rosenthal.
Virginia State Library: Edmund Randolph.

Page 17. Independence National Historical Park Collection: John Adams, by C. W. Peale.
Virginia State Library: William Grayson.

Page 23. Independence National Historical Park Collection: George Washington, by James Peale.

Page 45. Independence National Historical Park Collection: Thomas Jefferson, by C. W. Peale.

Page 64. Shelburne Museum: Patrick Henry.

Page 80. Independence National Historical Park Collection: Alexander Hamilton, by C. W. Peale.

Page 101. Independence National Historical Park Collection: Oliver Ellsworth, attributed to Sharples.

Page 136. Independence National Historical Park Collection: Rossiter's painting of the signing of the Constitution.

216

INDEX

221